NEW DIRECTIONS FOR HIGHER EDUCATION

Martin Kramer
EDITOR-IN-CHIEF

Understanding the Role of Academic and Student Affairs Collaboration in Creating a Successful Learning Environment

Adrianna Kezar
University of Maryland, College Park
Deborah J. Hirsch
University of Massachusetts Boston
Cathy Burack
University of Massachusetts Boston

EDITORS

Number 116, Winter 2001

JOSSEY-BASS
San Francisco

UNDERSTANDING THE ROLE OF ACADEMIC AND STUDENT AFFAIRS
COLLABORATION IN CREATING A SUCCESSFUL LEARNING ENVIRONMENT
Adrianna Kezar, Deborah J. Hirsch, Cathy Burack (eds.)
New Directions for Higher Education, no. 116
Martin Kramer, Editor-in-Chief

Microfilm copies of issues and articles are available in 16mm and 35mm,
as well as microfiche in 105mm, through University Microfilms Inc., 300
North Zeeb Road, Ann Arbor, Michigan 48106-1346.

ISSN 0271-0560   electronic ISSN 1534-2883   ISBN 0-7879-5784-4

NEW DIRECTIONS FOR HIGHER EDUCATION is part of The Jossey-Bass
Higher and Adult Education Series and is published quarterly by Wiley
Subscription Services, Inc., a Wiley company, at Jossey-Bass, 989 Market
Street, San Francisco, California 94103-1741. Periodicals postage paid at
San Francisco, California, and at additional mailing offices. Postmaster:
Send address changes to New Directions for Higher Education, Jossey-
Bass, 989 Market Street, San Francisco, California 94103-1741

SUBSCRIPTIONS cost $60 for individuals and $131 for institutions, agencies,
and libraries. See ordering information page at end of book.

EDITORIAL CORRESPONDENCE should be sent to the Editor-in-Chief,
Martin Kramer, 2807 Shasta Road, Berkeley, California 94708-2011.

Cover photograph and random dot by Richard Blair/Color & Light
© 1990.

Jossey-Bass Web address: www.josseybass.com

Printed in the United States of America on acid-free recycled paper con-
taining 100 percent recovered waste paper, of which at least 20 percent is
postconsumer waste.

CONTENTS

EDITORS' NOTES

There is no imperative as pressing in the twenty-first century as collaboration. This can be attributed to two main reasons: (1) the recognition of power in collaboration over individualism and (2) the necessity of collaboration for worldwide stability. Prominent examples such as Ghandi uniting the people of India for independence illustrated the power of collaboration, showing that almost anything can be overcome—even a world power set on control and dominance. The recognition of interdependence among people throughout the world has changed views about the need to work with others to accomplish mutual goals. The Internet and World Wide Web made this interconnection real and visible for many, with an international interconnection that has extended beyond anyone's wildest dreams. The potential and power of collaboration remains unrealized and is one of the primary challenges of this century.

Within this context, almost every sector is rethinking its organizational structure and work. Governments are striving to understand how conflicts can be resolved and how countries can work together (Torbet, 1994). Policymakers realize that their initiatives will not be accurate or implementable without input from communities. Environmentalists have made us aware that unless each country, state, or local area is involved in resolving water and air pollution, there is no hope for cleaning up waste. Businesses understand that their survival is based on strategic alliances and partnerships. Health care professionals strive to cure rare diseases and to improve health care through joint efforts across hospital and clinic borders. There is no sector in our society where collaboration is not discussed, attempted, and at times, accomplished. A simple search on collaboration in any library will turn up thousands of books across almost every conceivable discipline, the majority of which have been written in the last five years. Increasingly, academics, policymakers, entrepreneurs, and professionals are realizing that the issues that they care about—inventing a miraculous product, improving inner-city schools, protecting animals on the verge of extinction, saving a unique business—cannot be accomplished without partnerships. Corporate America, once a bastion of individualism, now focuses on collaboration; companies that foster collaboration are rising in the marketplace, whereas companies with individualistic bureaucratic organizations are failing. As a society, we now appear to understand the importance of collaboration. But we know little about how to collaborate successfully.

Not surprisingly, leaders have taken a keen interest in collaboration. In fact, Jean Lipman-Blumen (1996) suggests that the primary leadership challenge for the twenty-first century is to balance interdependence and diversity. A series of social, political, and economic forces necessitate collaboration, yet

1

deep divisions drive us apart and foil efforts to collaborate. Leaders are called upon to balance these forces. Collaboration is not only necessary in order to accomplish critical mutual goals; it is also a key factor in teamwork.

Working in teams has become the norm within most organizations. In the 1980s, most business experts were calling for greater cross-divisional work and teams in order to improve organizations and create excellence. During this period, teamwork was "good" operations and a part of the many new corporate fads such as total quality management. Today, the notion of teams has evolved to an overall ethic of collaboration that includes everything from partnering with outside groups to developing alliances to conflict management. Clearly, the development of teams and more group work in organizations was an important precursor to collaboration. But collaboration entails more than teams—it requires more work with diverse individuals and a strategic approach.

What does collaboration look like in higher education? The dialogue about collaboration has been ongoing in higher education for the last ten years. It began with discussions about the importance of teams and new notions about team leadership (see Bensimon and Neumann, 1993). It evolved into discussions about cross-divisional work through the introduction of total quality management (McGrath, 1998; Pickering and Hanson, 2000). But many academics simply saw teams and teamwork as a passing management fad.

Talk of collaboration, however, has not only been part of the administrative side of higher education. Many academics are leading the charge to develop cross-disciplinary programs and departments, to teach in learning communities, and to focus on group projects rather than individual learning (Torbet, 1994). The individualistic culture of the academy is not often friendly to calls for working in groups, shared goals, multidisciplinary teaching, or cross-divisional work. Yet, tenaciously, collaboration has continued to insert itself into campus discussions. Movements have included service learning, K–16 partnerships, collaborative and cooperative learning, industry partnerships, and partnerships between community and college. In addition, educational leaders have promoted the importance of collaboration across functional areas such as academic and student affairs. One of the most compelling reasons for higher education to change—and which propels this dialogue to continue—is that the outside world is changing: businesses, policymakers, and professionals are beginning to conduct their work differently. Higher education must prepare students for this new environment. If we cannot model this behavior, it is doubtful that we can prepare students to succeed in this new collaborative environment.

This volume synthesizes the calls for collaboration between academic and student affairs over the last decade. But most important, this volume begins to look at how we can collaborate successfully. As noted, there is a plethora of literature on the importance of collaborations and on the challenges that people trying to collaborate face, but few people have articulated what can lead to successful collaborations, especially within an academic context in which the culture of individuality makes working together even more difficult. Missing from the literature are research and examples of institutions that have been successful in developing collaborations between academic and student affairs. It is time to move beyond rhetoric to describing promising practices.

Although not a new subject, the topic of collaboration between academic and student affairs is now more important than ever if colleges and universities are to educate students for the new collaborative environment. We must show students by our own behavior that we believe in the power of collaboration, while still acknowledging that partnerships can be messy, that they can take more time, and that they can be frustrating. Authentic models of collaboration will help to develop successful student leaders for the new century. This volume focuses on providing institutions with information needed in order to develop collaboration between academic and student affairs on their campus, building on earlier work such as the American Association for Higher Education (AAHE), National Association of Student Personnel Administrators (NASPA), and American College Personnel Association's (ACPA) joint document, *Powerful Partnerships: A Shared Responsibility for Learning,* (1998).

In Chapter One, Donna Bourasa and Kevin Kruger review NASPA's and ACPA's involvement in fostering student and academic affairs partnerships during the last decade. This chapter summarizes the work of national organizations to foster this movement and suggests future directions for partnerships. As campuses contemplate partnerships, they can learn tremendous lessons from model institutions and practices that have evolved over the last decade. The chapter ends with a reprint of *Powerful Partnerships*. This report contains ten principles about learning and collaboration that can be used to frame discussions about partnerships on your campus.

Building on this historical knowledge, Adrianna Kezar in Chapter Two summarizes the results of a national study of academic and student affairs that examined reasons for collaboration, number of institutions engaged in the partnerships and types of collaboration, successful approaches, and barriers to and facilitators of collaboration. This chapter helps readers understand the current landscape of student and academic affairs collaboration. Campuses can use the empirical data about strategies for creating partnerships in their planning efforts to balance campus dialogue and generate enthusiasm (cultural strategies) with planning and restructuring (structural strategies).

Deborah J. Hirsch and Cathy Burack in Chapter Three also review strategies related to creating partnerships. Conversations with academic and student affairs officers at regional think tanks have improved institutional efforts to make needed transformations. The road to collaboration begins by uncovering the issues that are natural links between student and academic affairs. Assessment, technology, changing student population, student retention, and general education are areas around which campuses can build collaboration. Partnerships vary in form; Hirsch and Burack describe several possibilities, including restructuring, curricular innovations, and programmatic activities.

In Chapter Four, Kezar presents the results of a research study, identifying structural and cultural strategies for achieving collaboration between academic and student affairs staff. The results of a national survey reveal the critical role of leadership, cross-institutional dialogue, setting expectations, developing a common vision and language, generating enthusiasm, and planning. A combination of Kuh's model for change (proposed in earlier work) and planned change is recommended for facilitating collaboration between academic and student affairs. Chapter Five elaborates on these findings by drawing on the experiences of campuses.

Thara Fuller and Adrian Haugabrook describe in Chapter Five a campus-based strategy designed to facilitate collaboration. They examine the process of restructuring a division of student affairs as an educational partner with academic affairs and describe four collaborative efforts: the Beacon Leadership Project (a credit-bearing student-leadership development program), the Beacon Think Tank, the Diversity Research Initiative, and the Service Learning program. These programs demonstrate key ingredients of successful partnerships: relationships between key individuals, communication through formal and informal channels, shared language, combining resources, restructuring, cross-campus dialogues, team building, and shared mission.

In Chapter Six, the volume moves beyond ways of creating partnerships to methods for sustaining them. James Martin and James Samels present the results of a study with chief student affairs officers. The lessons learned illustrate that partnerships must be more strategic if they are to be sustained over time. Successful partnerships take an opportunistic approach, commit ongoing financial resources, manage staff turnover, mitigate culture clashes, link to campus assessment, publicize their successes, obtain board-level support, and are ready to close projects that do not work.

A complement to Martin and Samels's research on sustaining successful programs is Chapter Seven, Richard Guarasci's case study of a multifaceted program at Wagner College in New York. The key to this collaboration is its focus on student learning. The program connects students, student affairs administrators, and faculty to build a comprehensive approach, preparing students for participation in a democracy. Faculty and staff draw on the college's urban location in designing a program that joins learning communities, community-based learning, diversity education, and multidisciplinary studies.

The final chapter offers a fresh perspective on developing partnerships from the vantage point of a brand new campus. As a new institution, the Franklin W. Olin College of Engineering did not have to overcome the constraints of an existing separation between academic and student affairs. The authors of Chapter Eight had the opportunity to think about how a campus might be structured and organized to be learning and student centered.

Crafts, First, and Satwitz describe their experiences building a full partnership between academic and student affairs.

A number of common themes cut across the chapters in this volume. The most important is the way that collaboration enriches students' learning experience. As Crafts, First, and Satwitz note in Chapter Eight, "the blend of academics and extra- and cocurricular activities at Olin [College] makes learning more enjoyable and more pervasive and will ensure that . . . students have many more opportunities to learn than would otherwise be possible." *Powerful Partnerships,* the appendix to Chapter One, reminds readers that partnerships are necessary for learning—to connect classroom learning to life, to make learning more active, to relate past and present, and to capitalize on informal and incidental learning. As Martin and Samels point out, this learning is a strategic lever for developing partnerships that are sustainable and should be publicized widely. Hirsch and Burack's chapter helps the reader understand the ways in which partnerships have already been empirically proven to contribute to retention. We need to promote these ideas on our campuses.

Enriched learning experience ties to another theme—assessment. Hirsch and Burack note that within the climate of accountability on most campuses, assessment of learning is becoming more prevalent. Assessment not only provides a link with academic affairs; it also offers an opportunity for demonstrating the power and potential of seamless programs. The more evidence that can be amassed about the effectiveness of these programs, the more likely partnerships will increase as a priority on campus. Martin and Samels make us aware that "savvy student affairs officers . . . [forge] early connections between the objectives of their coventures and the published outcome assessment goals of the overall institution." Kezar illustrates in Chapter Two that although some campuses are assessing their student and academic partnerships, many more need to be involved with this practice. *Powerful Partnerships* reminds us that learning must be assessed in order for it to be developed. Olin College, described in Chapter Eight, provides a strong model for how such assessment should take place—across divisions and always focused on learning outcomes.

Assessment should not only be focused on the learning objectives; it should also connect to the institutional mission. Guarasci observes that the antidote to separate and competing divisions is an institutional mission with a shared educational practice. Fuller and Haugabrook describe a collaboration that could not have taken place if the partnership were not connected to the institution's mission. At the University of Massachusetts Boston, the shared mission provided an important place to begin dialogues. Discussions about how partnerships can enhance the institutional mission are critical for the formation and sustaining of these programs. As Martin and Samels note, if a partnership no longer fits within the institutional mission, then the institution should consider dissolving it. Partnerships need to be aligned with the central direction of the institution.

The majority of chapters describe community-service learning and learning communities as pedagogical innovations that have created opportunities for partnerships. The literature touts these as some of the best models for academic and student affairs partnerships. As Hirsch and Burack note, community-service learning and learning communities have already been proven to enhance learning and increase retention. Service-learning and learning-communities programs described in *Powerful Partnerships* demonstrate that these innovations enhance learning by making it active, capitalizing on incidental learning, articulating connections for students, and engaging the whole student. In Kezar's review of a national research study (Chapter Four), learning communities and community-service learning are among the most common and most successful partnerships. Fuller and Haugabrook's description of a service-learning program and Guarasci's model for a learning community offer readers detailed information about how these partnerships can be created. These models have many benefits: they are often well-funded, they have institutional structures to support them, and they have buy-in from members of the campus because of their visibility in education literature the last few decades.

Another theme that cuts across chapters concerns the ways to sustain and institutionalize programs. Institutional structures and resources are necessary to support partnerships over the long haul. Fuller and Haugabrook's chapter points to institutional resources and an effective organizational structure as underlying components of success. Martin and Samels state that "the greatest source of failure . . . continues to be a lack of financial support." They also argue that an institution's entire hierarchy, including the board of trustees, must provide support to partnerships. Hirsch and Burack describe the ways in which reorganizing and restructuring may be necessary to sustain partnerships in the long term. They note that conditions as simple as "shared space can foster the development of friendships and mutual respect among both academic and nonacademic colleagues." Kezar notes in Chapter Two that student affairs staff are likely to underestimate the importance of restructuring, planning, setting expectations and other strategies that are important for making sustainable partnerships. In addition, planning and restructuring are even more important at larger institutions. Crafts, First, and Satwicz provide an example of the way a campus can look when structures and resources are fully committed to partnerships.

Although concrete efforts such as structures and resources solidify partnerships, contributors also underscored the importance of informal interactions and planning for opportunistically creating partnerships. Serendipitous encounters and informal conversations provide the seeds for future collaboration. Martin and Samels implore institutions to be fluid and nimble, to be open to new ideas. A chance encounter may result in an extremely powerful future partnership. Hirsch and Burack's chapter speaks to the importance of conversations, which are more likely when student and academic offices share physical space. Campuses may want to consider ways to create more opportunities for informal interactions, such as social events or campus reading groups. As Crafts, First, and Satwicz illustrate, on a campus where many informal interactions occur, the dean can more easily find faculty for orientation and the student affairs staff will more easily find themselves in the classroom at faculty's request.

Various chapters review the importance of interpersonal dynamics (Fuller and Haugabrook, Kezar [Chapters Two and Four]), hiring new people (Kezar [Chapter Two]), and addressing the rapid turnover of student affairs staff (Martin and Samels) as necessary when building partnerships. In Chapter Two, Kezar points to impact of individual personalities and interpersonal interaction on the success of partnerships. As Fuller and Haugabrook describe, "much of the actual work of collaboration boils down to team building and attending to the individual relationships behind the larger partnerships." Martin and Samels provide an important cautionary note: if partnerships are relationship based, the rapid turnover of student affairs staff often hampers the developing and sustaining of partnerships. Institutions should better prepare for staff turnover in the development of partnerships so that faculty and academic affairs staff do not become frustrated. On the other hand, hiring new people can present opportunities to develop new partnerships.

Readers should heed the lessons learned from research and practice. These include focusing on learning and student centeredness, using successful models such as learning communities, capitalizing on chance opportunities, building in institutional resources and structural support, being attentive to relationships, and using assessment tools to evaluate both the program and the partnership. In their analyses of research and programmatic examples, the authors are unanimous in pointing to these actions as the elements of successful partnerships. Therefore, it is particularly important that campuses share the findings presented in this volume with staff while beginning partnerships.

References

American Association for Higher Education, American College Personnel Association, and National Association of Student Personnel Administrators. *Powerful Partnerships: A Shared Responsibility for Learning.* Washington, D.C.: American Association for Higher Education, American College Personnel Association, and National Association of Student Personnel Administrators, 1998.

Bensimon, E., and Neumann, A. *Redesigning Collegiate Leadership.* Baltimore, Md.: Johns Hopkins University Press, 1993.

Lipman-Blumen, J. *Connective Leadership.* San Francisco: Jossey-Bass, 1996.

McGrath, D. *Creating and Benefiting from Institutional Collaboration: Models for Success.* New Directions for Community Colleges, no. 103. San Francisco: Jossey-Bass, 1998.

Pickering, J., and Hanson, G. *The Collaboration Between Student Affairs and Institutional Researchers to Improve Institutional Effectiveness.* New Directions for Institutional Research, no. 108. San Francisco: Jossey-Bass, 2000.

Torbet, W. *Creating a Community of Inquiry: Conflict, Collaboration, and Transformation.* New York: Wiley, 1994.

ADRIANNA KEZAR is assistant professor in the higher education administration program at the University of Maryland, College Park.

DEBORAH J. HIRSCH is director of the New England Resource Center for Higher Education, University of Massachusetts Boston.

CATHY BURACK is associate director of the New England Resource Center for Higher Education, University of Massachusetts Boston.

1

In the last decade reported collaborations between student and academic affairs have increased and broadened.

The National Dialogue on Academic and Student Affairs Collaboration

Donna M. Bourassa and Kevin Kruger

It often seems that the student personnel profession has been writing and talking about issues of collaboration between student affairs and other sectors on campus since its very beginnings. Schroeder (1999) and Roberts (1998) note that collaboration issues were a central discussion of the 1949 *Student Personnel Point of View.* Jane Fried in *Steps to Creative Collaboration* (2000) captures the struggle the profession has faced in advancing this critical ideal: "By creating a common language in which we can discuss differences, we can begin to examine some of the frightening paradoxes of teaching and learning which have paralyzed our youth and trapped us all in 'parallel silos' on campus" (p. 9). As noted by Schroeder (1999), there is abundant literature that supports the challenges and obstacles in successful partnerships between academic and student affairs. These obstacles have primarily been seen as cultural differences, the historical separation between the formal curriculum and the informal curriculum, the perception of student affairs as an ancillary function to the academic mission, competing assumptions about the nature of student learning, and differential reward systems for faculty and student affairs professionals.

Role of Associations

Fiscal pressures and new literature have created a generation of new initiatives that challenge these obstacles. The need to do "more with less" in times of financial hardship led many institutions to expand the role of faculty into areas that were traditionally the purview of student affairs. This in

NEW DIRECTIONS FOR HIGHER EDUCATION, no. 116, Winter 2001   © Wiley Periodicals, Inc.

turn created new opportunities for collaboration between student affairs and academic affairs (Martin and Murphy, 2000). The trend toward restructuring in higher education led to many student affairs divisions reporting to academic affairs. This restructuring model also created new opportunities for collaboration.

The scholarly journals, publications, and conference presentations of the American College Personnel Association (ACPA) and the National Association of Student Personnel Administrators (NASPA) have advocated the need for collaboration between student affairs and academic affairs for over a decade. For most of that time there has not been a comparable movement in academic professional associations. "Those in academic affairs are preoccupied with their own challenges: assessment of learning outcomes, calls for Continuous Quality Improvement strategies, student 'consumerism,' the introduction of service learning initiatives, the need for remediation and the popularity of remote learning, to name just a few" (Martin and Murphy, 2000, p. 5).

In their roles as the leading associations for student affairs professionals, NASPA and ACPA have focused their curriculum on the importance of student and academic affairs collaboration for over ten years. A review of programs presented during both the ACPA and NASPA annual conferences from 1991 to 2001 reveals that professional attention to academic–student affairs collaboration grew from a small item of interest to a major focus during that time. Much of the dialogue in the early 1990s was program specific, with few suggesting a comprehensive campus-wide approach to collaboration. These early efforts were also one-sided in nature and described involving faculty in student affairs programs, without a parallel involvement of student affairs professionals in the academic arena. Largely, the innovations cited were of individual faculty participating in residence hall programs or career workshops. These early programs suggest that the institutional climate was not ready to support either broad strategic initiatives to involve faculty in traditional student affairs programs or efforts to involve student affairs staff in traditional areas of the curriculum.

Several documents supported by ACPA and NASPA began to change the intellectual climate in ways that opened the door to more comprehensive collaborations on campus. These documents shifted the dialogue from single-program initiatives based on the personalities and relationships between individual faculty and student affairs staff members to campus-based programs that recognized the complexity of the student learning process and the key role student affairs staff played in that process. The *Student Learning Imperative* (American College Personnel Association, 1994), *Reasonable Expectations* (National Association of Student Personnel Administrators, 1995) and *Principles of Good Practice* (National Association of Student Personnel Administrators, 1997) were critical documents in transforming the dialogue around this critical topic.

The change in the dialogue set the stage for a major collaboration between the American Association for Higher Education (AAHE), ACPA, and NASPA, which culminated in their joint publication of *Powerful Partnerships: A Shared Responsibility for Learning* (1998). The involvement of AAHE in this project propelled academic and student affairs collaboration into a "front-burner" issue for both faculty and student affairs faculty and staff on campus. The effect of *Powerful Partnerships*, which is reprinted as an appendix to this chapter, has been significant. The ten-year review of conference programs for ACPA and NASPA reveals a significant increase in the type and number of programs presented. During the 2000 ACPA and NASPA conferences, a total of 42 programs focused on issues related to collaboration between academic and student affairs compared to six in 1991.

Themes of Collaboration

A review of the content of the forty-two programs to be presented during the ACPA and NASPA conferences in 2002 revealed a number of themes that shed light on the approaches that campuses are using to address academic and student affairs collaboration. The programs that will be presented during these conferences represent a glimpse at the curriculum of the two associations and as such indicate the state of innovation in academic and student affairs collaborations. The following themes emerged.

Faculty-in-Residence Programs. Many of the early innovations in academic–student affairs collaboration came through the simple act of inviting faculty to participate in residence hall programs and activities. Over the last decade these programs have evolved to more substantial involvement with resident students at four-year institutions. The marked increase in academically themed housing and emphasis placed on the living-learning nature of the residence experience has led to the development of a significant number of comprehensive faculty-in-residence programs. The residential experience provides limitless opportunities for integrating the student academic experience with out-of-class experience. Many small colleges now institute a "great works" program that provides cohorts of residence students with the opportunity to have faculty and staff facilitate literature discussions from class during their time in the residence hall.

First-Year Experience. First-year programs have been easy candidates for building collaborative relationships. Involvement of faculty in orientation has traditionally been the most nominal example of these efforts. More programs now involve faculty in teaching or facilitating University 101 courses, and faculty are now playing significant roles in programs that support at-risk students during their first year.

Learning Communities. Perhaps one of the richest areas for collaboration has been on campuses that have focused their efforts on improving the climate for student learning on campus. The establishment of freshmen interest groups is a powerful example of how academic and student affairs collaboration can improve the experience of student learning on campus. At campuses such as the University of Missouri, over 70 percent of students are now participating in living-learning communities that involve significant collaboration between academic and student affairs faculty and staff.

Student Life Programs. Scores of innovative programs involving faculty in traditional student affairs activities have developed in the last five years. Examples include programs that involve faculty in honor councils, programs for students with disabilities, faculty mentoring programs, career development, and diversity programming.

The College Student. Student affairs professionals are in a position to understand the unique nature of both traditional and nontraditional college students. Increasingly, collaborative programs have been developed that involve student affairs professionals in faculty development and training programs. The recent concern about the nature of the "millennial student" has created opportunities for campuses such as the University of Central Florida to work collaboratively with faculty in developing learning strategies for today's student.

Academic–Student Affairs Planning Teams. Arguably, the best models for collaboration exist when the collaboration efforts are more than one-time, single-program initiatives on campus. The strongest models today include planning teams that coordinate and emphasize the need for collaborative programs. Programs such as the Collaborative Action Team (CAT) at the University of Arkansas are good examples of a strategic approach to planning campus-based collaboration.

The Current Landscape

We conducted an informal survey with a small number of student affairs practitioners and scholars who have been actively engaged in advancing the knowledge and practices of academic and student affairs collaboration. Our inquiry focused on three key questions that are widely discussed whenever the topic of academic–student affairs collaboration is at the forefront:

1. Over the past ten years has the dialogue concerning student affairs and academic affairs collaboration changed? If yes, in what ways?
2. In looking at the higher education landscape, what are the obstacles to successful implementation of student affairs and academic affairs collaborations on campus?
3. What do you see as the future for student and academic affairs collaboration/partnerships?

Several important themes emerged from the responses of the senior leadership of these associations, including the following: significant changes have taken place regarding the nature of the collaborations between student and academic affairs; the obstacles and opportunities are still largely enmeshed in the necessity of each entity to deepen their understanding of the other's culture; the community college perspective warrants further consideration; and assessment will play a critical role in advancing successful, sustainable collaborative ventures between student and academic affairs.

Progress Clearly Demarcated

In reflecting on the preceding questions, respondents uniformly conveyed their belief that major inroads in aligning the values and expectations of both groups have been made, lessening the notion that the two groups are working at cross-purposes. One respondent wrote: "I recall the dialogue ten years ago to be one of support to the academic experience or services and programs referred to as 'extracurricular' activities. While significant to the student experience, these efforts were often separate and, in many cases, disconnected from the academic focus of the institution. I think that current practices are more 'seamless' and our connection and role in the learning-centered institution is better defined and more deliberate. . . . Many student affairs units now have mission statements that fully complement the institution's mission resulting in consistent campus goals."

Another respondent expressed similar sentiments and underscored the changing nature of the dialogue in spurring student affairs to perceive themselves as full partners in the learning enterprise:

> Previously, the dialogue was dominated by notions of inferiority and striving for acceptance in the academy. Journal articles and conference presentations focused on the inferior relationship of student affairs in relation to academic affairs, citing equal contributions of the out-of-class environment to student learning. We have moved from the rhetoric of inferiority to a deeper understanding of our contribution to student learning both in and outside of the classroom. We have accepted that part of our role is to support student learning in very fundamental ways through academic support. We have realized that this cannot only be the work of a single department, but must be a part the work of multiple functional areas. The introduction of the *Student Learning Imperative* was pivotal in changing the nature of the dialogue.

Top Priority: Blending Two Distinct Cultures

Much has been written about the existing cultural traditions, norms, and attitudes defining both student affairs and the ivory towers of the academy. Engstrom and Tinto (2000, pp. 429–430) provide an extremely useful table summarizing the perceived differences of these two distinct entities in terms of their traditional cultural characteristics, norms, and attitudes. For example, the culture within student affairs is one that fosters working collaboratively, in groups, to solve problems, whereas faculty engage in solitary, autonomous work. Both groups hold a different perception of students' role in decision making—student affairs seeks student involvement, and faculty believe they know what is best for the students. Among our respondents, resolving cultural differences remains the top priority. The following narratives eloquently describe the points of tension:

> Regardless of the type of governance system, another obstacle is faculty and student affairs cultures; they are so different that sometimes simple communication is difficult, let alone, program planning and implementation. One related area that is always raised as an obstacle is the faculty reward system. In my experience, if the faculty and student affairs staff are committed to a project and enjoy working together, the reward system is rarely a problem.

> On my campus, most collaboration is done between high-level administrators, making few meaningful opportunities for entry or mid-level staff to collaborate with faculty. I also think that student affairs needs to do a better job at reaching out to faculty and promoting themselves in a variety of ways. I don't think that the typical faculty member devalues student affairs, but I don't think they know much about student affairs. Student affairs administrators also need lessons in faculty life. We need to know how faculty members structure their time and the various elements of the promotion and tenure process.

Although these obstacles seem formidable, Engstrom and Tinto (2000) lay out a multitude of strategies that can give rise to innovative types of partnerships emerging to create seamless learning environments. These strategies are tied to ways to modify or adapt institutional governances structures, reward systems, and faculty and staff development programs, to name a few. The authors also provide specific organizational models and best practices that spur transformative shifts in the way institutions opt to achieve learning-centered communities.

Tracking the Two-Year College Perspective

To date, much of the literature on student and academic affairs collaboration has focused on the four-year institution. Of late, the way in which these collaborative practices occur between students and academic affairs at public two-year colleges has received increased prominence, as evidenced by NASPA's selection of its 2000 Dissertation of the Year Award. The recipient, Craig Kolins, authored a dissertation titled, "An appraisal of collaboration: Assessing perceptions of chief academic and student affairs officers at public two-year colleges" (1999). Kolins presented his findings that year at both the NASPA and ACPA annual meetings.

Kolins surveyed senior-level administrators from 327 two-year public colleges "to determine and compare CAO [chief academic affairs officer] and

CSAO [chief student affairs officer] perceptions about (a) the frequency of collaboration; (b) the level of collaboration; and (c) the importance of collaboration in enhancing student success and (d) their satisfaction with collaboration" (1999, p. iii). The study included the following significant findings: a large number of collaborative practices occurred between student and academic affairs at community colleges, both CAOs and CSAOs perceive collaboration as important to enhancing student success, both groups were satisfied with the collaborations that occurred at their institutions, and both groups perceived their collaborative relationships with each other as discordant but not conflicting.

The receptivity of the community college sector to engage in collaboration may be due in part to the institutions' organizational structure or where the reporting line is for student affairs units. Findlen (2000) notes that smaller two-year colleges increasingly are merging the chief of academic affairs and student affairs into one position. Similarly, the 1996 NASPA national survey of CSAOs on the state of restructuring in student affairs found that some community colleges are more likely to combine or integrate academic and student affairs units.

Without a doubt, the entire higher education community should keep track of factors within the community college sector that cultivate successful partnerships that are easily adapted by either community colleges or four-year colleges and universities. For example, the community college sector is leading the way in the formation of strong, vibrant student and academic affairs partnerships as well as partnerships with external constituencies in the development and advancement of educational outcomes tied to service learning.

Assessment of Student and Academic Affairs Collaborations

Researchers and practitioners have begun to articulate what needs to come next in order to strengthen the likelihood of successful collaborations. Schroeder (1999) identifies a comprehensive agenda for future research, providing the reader with a comprehensive list of twenty questions requiring further study. These research questions suggest examination of topics such as determining the extent "would-be" collaborators know and agree on the desired goals and outcomes for their particular collaborative partnership, identifying the skills and competencies needed for educators to shift to collaborative functioning, and ascertaining the social, political, economic, and moral implications of collaboration.

As higher education heeds the public cry for greater accountability, campus collaborations will continue to receive much more national visibility. Few collaborative efforts have been evaluated in a manner that actually demonstrates that significant benefits occur in advancing higher education's overall mission. One respondent to our survey conveys a sense of optimism:

"Much more attention is being given to assessment of the collaborative approaches. Academic offices and faculty are showing greater interest. I am optimistic that these collaborations will grow and flourish in new areas, especially as assessment data and evidence is gathered that supports their contribution to student learning."

As chair of the national task force on collaboration that authored *Powerful Partnerships: A Shared Responsibility for Learning,* David Potter (1999) reminds us that becoming a more learning-centered university "obligates us to imagine and establish more powerful learning environments, assessing their power not by their characteristics but by how much learning occurs in them" (p. 16). Therefore, there must be a common language between student affairs staff, faculty, and campus administrators in delineating the desired student learning outcomes.

Role of Professional Associations in the Future

ACPA, NASPA, and AAHE invested both resources and time into *Powerful Partnerships* in 1997 and 1998. Following the success of this initiative, ACPA and NASPA partnered with the Educational Resources Information Center (ERIC) to sponsor a follow-up study on the experiences of senior student affairs officers in developing collaborations with academic affairs. The results of this research study are presented in Chapters Two, Three, and Four of the present volume.

ACPA and NASPA have produced several critical documents over the past seven years that now serve as an important foundation for the advancement of academic and student affairs collaborations:

- *The Student Learning Imperative* (American College Personnel Association, 1994)
- *Reasonable Expectations* (National Association of Student Personnel Administrators, 1995)
- *Powerful Partnerships: A Shared Responsibility for Learning* (American Association for Higher Education, American College Personnel Association, and National Association of Student Personnel Administrators, 1998)
- *Collaboration and Partnerships* (Schroeder, 1999)
- *Steps to Creative Campus Collaboration* (Fried, 2000)
- *Building a Better Bridge: Creating Effective Partnerships Between Academic Affairs and Student Affairs* (Martin and Murphy, 2001)

In addition, an exploratory committee has been formed between ACPA, NASPA, and AAHE to begin plans for *Powerful Partnerships II.*

Central to their mission, professional associations make choices as to which issues will feature prominently in the generation and dissemination of new knowledge and educational training and professional development programs (Nuss, 2000). The notion of "out of sight, out of mind" often plagues student affairs professionals; therefore, associations must stay vigilant in promulgating the necessity for, and benefits of, collaboration. Clearly, professional associations will continue to be both barometers *of* and advocates *for* the collaborations between academic and student affairs.

References

American Association for Higher Education, American College Personnel Association, and National Association of Student Personnel Administrators. *Powerful Partnerships: A Shared Responsibility for Learning.* Washington, D.C.: American Association of Higher Education, American College Personnel Association, and National Association of Student Personnel Administrators, 1998

American College Personnel Association. *The Student Learning Imperative: Implications for Student Affairs.* Washington, D.C.: American College Personnel Association, 1994.

American Council on Education. *The Student Personnel Point of View.* (Rev. ed.) American Council of Education Studies Series 6, vol. 13, no. 13). Washington, D.C.: American Council of Education, 1949.

Engstrom, C. M., and Tinto, V. "Developing Partnerships with Academic Affairs to Enhance Student Learning." In M. J. Barr, M. K. Desler, and Associates (eds.), *The Handbook of Student Affairs Administration.* San Francisco: Jossey-Bass, 2000.

Findlen, G. L. "A Dean's Survival Kit." In D. Robillard Jr. (ed.), *Dimensions of Managing Academic Affairs in Community College.* New Directions for Community Colleges, no. 109. San Francisco: Jossey-Bass, 2000.

Fried, J. *Steps to Creative Campus Collaboration.* Washington, D.C.: National Association of Student Personnel Administrators, 2000.

Kolins, C. A. "An Appraisal of Collaboration: Assessing Perceptions of Chief Academic and Student Affairs Officers at Public Two-Year Colleges." Unpublished doctoral dissertation, University of Toledo, 1999.

Martin, J., and Murphy, S. *Building a Better Bridge: Creating Effective Partnerships Between Academic Affairs and Student Affairs.* Washington, D.C.: National Association of Student Personnel Administrators, 2000.

National Association of Student Personnel Administrators. *Principles of Good Practice for Student Affairs.* Washington, D.C.: National Association of Student Personnel Administrators, 1997.

National Association of Student Personnel Administrators. *Reasonable Expectations.* Washington, D.C.: National Association of Student Personnel Administrators, 1995.

Nuss, E. M. "The Role of Professional Associations." In M. J. Barr, M. K. Desler, and Associates (eds.), *The Handbook of Student Affairs Administration.* San Francisco: Jossey-Bass, 2000.

Potter, D. L. "Where Powerful Partnerships Begin." *About Campus,* 1999, 4(2), 11–16.

Roberts, D. C. "Student Learning Was Always Supposed to Be the Core of Our Work: What Happened?" *About Campus,* 1998, 3(3), 18–22.

Schroeder, C. "Collaboration and Partnerships." In C. S. Johnson and H. E. Cheatham (eds.), *Higher Education Trends for the Next Century: A Research Agenda for Student Success.* Washington, D.C.: American College Personnel Association, 1999.

DONNA M. BOURASSA is the assistant executive director with the American College Personnel Association and has an adjunct faculty appointment at George Washington University.

KEVIN KRUGER is associate executive director of the National Association of Student Personnel Administrators. He was formally assistant vice president for student affairs at the University of Maryland, Baltimore County.

Powerful Partnerships: A Shared Responsibility for Learning: A Joint Report

Despite American higher education's success at providing collegiate education for an unprecedented number of people, the vision of equipping all our students with learning deep enough to meet the challenges of the post-industrial age provides us with a powerful incentive to do our work better. People collaborate when the job they face is too big, is too urgent, or requires too much knowledge for one person or group to do alone. Marshalling what we know about learning and applying it to the education of our students is just such a job. This report makes the case that only when everyone on campus—particularly academic affairs and student affairs staff—shares the responsibility for student learning will we be able to make significant progress in improving it.

Collectively, we know a lot about learning. A host of faculty, staff, and institutional initiatives undertaken since the mid-1980s and supported by colleges and universities, foundations, government, and other funding sources have resulted in a stream of improvement efforts related to teaching, curriculum, assessment, and learning environments. The best practices from those innovations and reforms mirror what scholars from a variety of disciplines, from neurobiology to psychology, tell us about the nature of learning. Exemplary practices are also shaped by the participants' particular experiences as learners and educators, which is why a program cannot simply be adopted but must be adapted to a new environment.

Despite these examples, most colleges and universities do not use their collective wisdom as well as they should. To do so requires a commitment to and support for action that goes beyond the individual faculty or staff member. Distracted by other responsibilities and isolated from others from whom they could learn about learning and who would support them, most people on campus contribute less effectively to the development of students' understanding than they might. It is only by acting cooperatively in the context of common goals, as the

American Association for Higher Education; American College Personnel Association; National Association of Student Personnel Administrators. June 1998. Reprinted with permission of the American College Personnel Association.

most innovative institutions have done, that our accumulated understanding about learning is put to best use.

There is another reason to work collaboratively to deepen student learning. Learning is a social activity, and modeling is one of the most powerful learning tools. As participants in organizations dedicated to learning, we have a responsibility to model for students how to work together on behalf of our shared mission and to learn from each other.

On behalf of such collaboration, we, the undersigned members of this Joint Task Force on Student Learning, offer the following report. It begins with a statement of the insights gained through the scholarly study of learning and their implications for pedagogy, curricula, learning environments, and assessment. Each principle is illustrated by a set of exemplary cooperative practices that bring together academic and student affairs professionals to make a difference in the quality of student learning, a difference that has been assessed and documented. The report ends with a call to all involved in higher education to reflect upon these findings and examples in conjunction with their own and their colleagues' experience and to draw on all these sources of knowledge as the basis for actions to promote higher student achievement.

Powerful Partnerships—Joint Task Force on Student Learning: A Shared Responsibility for Learning

The following ten principles about learning and how to strengthen it are drawn from research and practice and provide grounds for deliberation and action. All those who participate in the educational mission of institutions of higher education—students, faculty, and staff—share responsibility for pursuing learning improvements. Collaborations between academic and student affairs personnel and organizations have been especially effective in achieving this better learning for students. We advocate these partnerships as the best way to realize fully the benefits of the findings.

Learning Principles and Collaborative Action

1. Learning is fundamentally about *making and maintaining connections:* biologically through neural networks; mentally among concepts, ideas, and meanings; and experientially through interaction between the mind and the environment, self and other, generality and context, deliberation and action.

    Rich learning experiences and environments require and enable students to *make connections:*
    - through **learning materials** that stimulate comparisons and associations, explore relationships, evaluate alternative perspectives and solutions, and challenge students to draw conclusions from evidence;

- through opportunities to **relate** their **own experience** and knowledge **to materials** being learned;
- through **pedagogies** emphasizing critical analysis of conflicting views and demanding that students make defensible judgments about and demonstrate linkages among bodies of knowledge;
- through **curricula** integrating ideas and themes within and across fields of knowledge and establishing coherence among learning experiences within and beyond the classroom; and
- through **classroom** experiences **integrated with** purposeful **activities outside of class.**

To make and maintain connections, faculty and staff collaborators design learning experiences that:
- expose students to alternative world views and culturally diverse perspectives;
- give students responsibility for solving problems and resolving conflicts;
- make explicit the relationships among parts of the curriculum and between the curriculum and other aspects of the collegiate experience; and
- deliberately personalize interventions appropriate to individual students' circumstances and needs.

University of Maryland, College Park offers the College Park Scholars program, a two-year living/learning opportunity for freshmen and sophomores. Students reside and attend most of their classes within residence hall communities. Residence life staff, faculty, and other program staff offices are in the halls. Student scholars live on floors corresponding to thematically linked academic programs. For participating commuting students, access is provided to common areas in host residence halls. The thematic programs deliberately connect what the students learn in the classroom to the larger world through weekly colloquia, discussion groups, and field trips dealing with related issues.

The scholars program has improved recruitment and retention of talented undergraduates and has provided an enriched learning experience and a more personalized and human scale to campus life. Faculty offices and classrooms within the residence halls lead to enhanced interaction with faculty.

At *University of Missouri, Kansas City,* Supplemental Instruction and Video-Based Supplemental Instruction help students **make connections.** Supplemental Instruction uses peer-assisted study sessions to increase student academic performance and student retention in historically difficult academic courses. In the sessions, students learn how to integrate course content and develop reasoning and study strategies, facilitated by student leaders who have previously succeeded in these courses and who are trained in study strategies and peer collaborative learning techniques. The video-based program offers an alternative course delivery system. Faculty offer courses on videotape and students enroll in a video section. A facilitator guides review of the video lectures, stopping the tapes in mid-lecture to engage in class discussions, integration, and practice of learning strategies.

More than three hundred studies nationally have documented the impact of supplemental instruction, demonstrating its special impact on students with weak academic preparation. The U.S. Department of Education designated supplemental instruction as an Exemplary Education Program in 1982, noting its ability to increase academic achievement and college graduation rates among students. Program staff at UMKC have further investigated the effects of this instruction through the study of neurological processes. Using a Quantitative Electroencephalography instrument, they have found evidence of improved brain electrical activity in students who participate in the programs.

2. Learning is enhanced by *taking place in* the context of *a compelling situation* that balances challenge and opportunity, stimulating and utilizing the brain's ability to conceptualize quickly and its capacity and need for contemplation and reflection upon experiences.

Presenting students with *compelling situations* amplifies the learning process. Students learn more when they are:
- asked to tackle complex and compelling problems that invite them to develop an array of workable and innovative solutions;
- asked to produce work that will be shared with multiple audiences;
- offered opportunities for active application of skills and abilities and time for contemplation; and
- placed in settings where they can draw upon past knowledge and competencies while adapting to new circumstances.

To create compelling situations, faculty and staff collaborators:
- articulate and enforce high standards of student behavior inside and outside the classroom;
- give students increasing responsibility for leadership;
- create environments and schedules that encourage intensive activity as well as opportunities for quiet deliberation; and
- establish internships, externships, service-learning, study abroad, and workplace-based learning experiences.

The First-Year Experience at the *College of New Jersey* is a collaboration between General Education and Student Life. Students live in residence hall communities with a volunteer non-resident faculty fellow for each floor. Faculty fellows, student life staff, and students plan residence hall activities. Students also take an interdisciplinary core course, *Athens to New York,* taught by full-time faculty and selected student life staff in residence hall classrooms, and incorporating service-learning. Four questions drive the mission of the First-Year Experience: What does it mean to be human? What does it mean to be a member of a community? What does it mean to

be moral, ethical, and just? and How do communities respond to differences? Service-learning provides a **compelling situation** in which students
can confront complex social issues, apply their talents to marginalized communities, interact and work with diverse populations, and enhance their
career preparation.

Student service-learning journals show a clear understanding of the
work of the course and its objectives and core questions. Community
agency staff provide feedback and guidance to students, and the staffs' evaluations offer evidence that students learn about and contribute to their communities. Students express high levels of satisfaction with the residence hall,
the classroom experience, workshops, field trips, and enrichment lectures
associated with the core course.

Community College of Rhode Island's 2+4 Service on Common Ground
Program is part of the college's extensive service-learning activities. Supported by funds from the Campus Compact National Center for Community
Colleges and the Corporation for National Service to develop service-learning
partnerships between community colleges and four-year institutions, the college cooperates with Brown University's Center for Public Service. One joint
project connects the community college's nursing faculty and students with
the university's medical school faculty and students. Students work in many
challenging situations to meet community needs and discuss and write in
journals observations and experiences that relate the activity to their course
of study and to social issues.

Student affairs staff began the program with a core team of five faculty.
Now the collaborative effort includes some fifty faculty who employ service-
learning in more than a dozen academic disciplines.

3. Learning is an *active search for meaning* by the learner—constructing
   knowledge rather than passively receiving it, shaping as well as being
   shaped by experiences.

   Active participation by the learner is essential for productive learning, dictating that:
   - instructional methods **involve students directly** in the discovery of
     knowledge;
   - learning materials challenge students to **transform prior knowledge and
     experience** into new and deeper understandings;
   - students be expected to **take responsibility** for their own learning;
   - students be encouraged to **seek meaning** in the context of ethical **values
     and commitments;** and
   - learning be assessed based on students' ability to **demonstrate compe-
     tencies and use knowledge.**

   **To stimulate an active search for meaning, faculty and staff col-
   laborators:**
   - expect and demand student participation in activities in and beyond the
     classroom;

- design projects and endeavors through which students apply their knowledge and skills; and
- build programs that feature extended and increasingly challenging opportunities for growth and development.

Bloomfield College (New Jersey) offers the Student Advancement Initiative, curricular and co-curricular experiences that **develop student competencies** in aesthetic appreciation, communication, citizenship, cultural awareness, problem solving and critical thinking, science and technology, and other professional skills. The program emphasizes computer-aided self-appraisal for students and a student development transcript. The objectives are to **involve students actively** in the assessment process, to provide continuous feedback to students on their progress toward the competencies, and to strengthen programs based on aggregate information about student achievement of the competencies.

Faculty and student affairs joint task forces have defined the competencies and linked them to the general education program. Faculty draw upon student affairs staff expertise in designing course assignments. Student portfolios and assessment information direct students toward self-analysis and synthesis of theoretical and practical knowledge gained through the curriculum and through developmental activities. Faculty and staff participate together in "reflective practice" sessions to improve programming and administration.

DePaul University (Illinois) offers two writing-intensive interdisciplinary and experiential programs for new students to ease the transition to the university. All first-year students enroll in either Focal Point or Discover Chicago. Focal Point highlights an important event, person, place, or issue and is taught using a multidisciplinary format. Students also enroll in a "common hour" course where student affairs professionals **help students evaluate their contributions** to shared learning, develop their study and decision-making skills, create a learning plan, and reflect upon the nature of diversity at the university and in the city. Academic and student affairs personnel are involved in curriculum development, the design of classroom experiences, and student learning outside the classroom. Discover Chicago brings new students together a week before the first term for a course team-taught by a faculty member, a professional staff member, and a student mentor. The course investigates a particular topic using the city as a learning site. The work of the course involves readings and discussions, visits to city locations, and a community service project.

Assessments of the programs are designed to determine their impact on student retention and include qualitative and quantitative pre- and post-test surveys, a standardized test (the College Student Inventory) that is a predictor of student retention, syllabi review, and focus groups. Results provide information about retention and staff-faculty partnering, student expectations about the university and coursework, and the nature of assignments and forms of evaluation in each program.

4. Learning is *developmental,* a cumulative process *involving the whole person,* relating past and present, integrating the new with the old, starting from but transcending personal concerns and interests.

The *developmental* **nature of learning implies both a holistic and a temporal perspective on the learning process. This suggests that:**
- any **single** learning **experience** or instructional **method** has a **lesser** impact **than** the **overall** educational experience;
- **curricula** should be **additive and cumulative, building upon prior under-standings and knowledge** toward greater richness and complexity;
- intellectual **growth** is **gradual,** with periods of rapid **advancement fol-lowed by time for consolidation,** an extended and episodic process of mutually reinforcing experiences;
- the goals of undergraduate education should include students' **develop-ment of an integrated sense of identity,** characterized by high self-esteem and personal integrity that extends beyond the individual to the larger community and world; and
- **assessment of** learning should encompass **all aspects of** the educational experience.

To create a developmental process integrating all aspects of stu-dents' lives, faculty and staff collaborators:
- design educational programs to build progressively on each experience;
- track student development through portfolios that document levels of competence achieved and intentional activities leading to personal devel-opment;
- establish arenas for student-faculty interaction in social and community settings; and
- present opportunities for discussion and reflection on the meaning of all collegiate experiences.

Virginia Polytechnic Institute and State University attends to the overall health of students through its Wellness Environment for Living and Learn-ing. Students who participate make a commitment to a substance-free lifestyle and residence environment. Faculty and student affairs profession-als co-teach a wellness forum, a one-credit course in the residence halls in which undergraduate resident advisors also assist. Additional programming emphasizes **social, physical, intellectual, career, emotional, and spiritual purpose and philosophy.** A student-run community board enables students to develop programs and to take responsibility for managing the housing experience. Campus speakers share personal experiences with substance abuse and wellness issues, and faculty and student affairs staff relate their life experiences in class discussions. The residential community, hall pro-grams, and course curriculum encourage students to reflect on past behav-iors and to determine how new knowledge can assist them in college and in developing holistic approaches to a healthy life.

Participation in the program has increased dramatically in two years, with a significant rate of returning students and requests for additional residents. The first group of students had a significantly higher grade-point average than a control group in the beginning semester of the program.

University of Richmond (Virginia) provides a four-year experience at its women's residential college, the Women Involved in Living and Learning Program. Participants enroll in an interdisciplinary women's studies minor and in required gender-related educational programs. Goals include increasing self-awareness, self-confidence, independence, and leadership through structured educational experiences; stimulating critical thinking and analysis about gender roles and relationships; nurturing and promoting student potential and talent; fostering awareness and acceptance of difference; and providing students with curricular and co-curricular opportunities to inform and enhance academic, career, and life choices. The professional program coordinator works closely with the women's studies faculty to plan course offerings, serves on its advisory board, and teaches courses. Students complete a supervised internship and attend monthly membership meetings of a student-run organization and sponsored events that complement program goals. Events form the basis for **discussion and reflection in the courses and informally in the residence halls.**

Wellesley College's Center for Research on Women recently completed an assessment of this program using course effectiveness instruments, an annual survey to determine the overall impact, a self-esteem measure, an alumnae survey to evaluate the long-term program impact, and student focus groups. Results confirm the cumulative and developmental effects on participants. The study found the greatest effect on those who completed all four years of the program. Students and alumnae of the program speak of the transformational aspects of their involvement, the ways they learned to think critically that benefit them in diverse situations, their ability to question their own world views, and their tolerance of different viewpoints. Alumnae of the program express greater satisfaction with their undergraduate experience than non-program alumnae.

5. Learning is done by *individuals* who are intrinsically *tied to others as social beings,* interacting as competitors or collaborators, constraining or supporting the learning process, and able to enhance learning through cooperation and sharing.

The *individual and social nature of learning* has the potential for creating powerful learning environments that:
- take into account students' personal histories and common cultures;
- feature **opportunities for cooperative learning,** study, and shared research;
- cultivate a climate in which students see themselves as part of an **inclusive community;**

- use the **residential experience** as a resource for collaborative learning and for integrating social and academic life;
- use **school, work, home, and community** as resources for collaborative learning and for integrating social and academic life; and
- give students a chance to fathom and appreciate **human differences**.

To relate individuals to others as social beings, faculty and staff collaborators:

- strive to develop a campus culture where students learn to help each other;
- establish peer tutoring and student and faculty mentorship programs;
- sponsor residence hall and commuting student programs that cultivate student and faculty interaction for social and educational purposes; and
- support activities that enable students from different cultural backgrounds to experience each other's traditions.

The Program on Intergroup Relation, Conflict, and Community at the *University of Michigan, Ann Arbor* offers undergraduate coursework and co-curricular programming in several departments, emphasizing intergroup relations and using a variety of pedagogical approaches. Beginning as a faculty initiative, the program is managed and funded by the College of Literature, Science, and the Arts, and the Division of Student Affairs. Program features include:

- first-year departmental course seminars, linked through a faculty seminar and taught by faculty seminar and taught by faculty and student affairs teams and incorporating out-of-classroom experiences designed to build communities of students beyond the individual seminars;
- Intergroup Dialogues, two-credit courses **bringing together students from social identity groups** for intensive peer-facilitated dialogues based on integrated readings, discussions, and experiential exercises;
- facilitator training and practicum courses for Intergroup Dialogue leaders;
- advanced courses in intergroup relations in sociology and psychology;
- consultation and workshops by program staff working with university departments and offices, training programs for staff and organizations, and special campus events;
- a resource center on intergroup relations equipped with books, articles, and videos on related topics.

A current study of the program assessed a course that included required Intergroup Dialogues. The study found that the course increased students' structured thinking about racial and ethnic inequality, enabled them to apply this thinking more generally to social phenomena not explicitly covered in the course, and affected the kinds of actions students advocated in intergroup conflicts.

Portland State University (Oregon) faculty developed their general education program using research on student learning and retention and working with student affairs professionals with expertise in student learning, group dynamics, peer facilitation, and the development of community and feelings of inclusion. The program emphasizes **the integration of both affective and cognitive modes of learning** into all aspects of its classes. It strives to overcome the limited opportunity for informal learning and casual interaction characteristic of urban, commuter campuses. Features of the program include:

- CityQuest, an orientation program designed as an activity in a freshman general education course;
- a "leadership cluster" of multidisciplinary upper-division courses on leadership fulfilling general education requirements;
- student affairs fellows who teach in the "freshman inquiry" and "senior capstone" courses;
- Metro Initiative, cooperative agreements with regional community colleges that connect academic support services and general education coursework across all institutions;
- Capstone, a collaboration to facilitate service-learning within the general education curriculum; and
- Student Snapshot, a student affairs newsletter with information about students to help faculty understand students' lives.

Since implementation of the program, student retention between the first and second year has increased, the institution has developed a better sense of who its students are, and it has information on which aspects of students' learning experiences are more or less effective. Faculty are now more likely to request assistance with students from student affairs staff and to involve the staff in teaching program courses.

6. Learning is strongly *affected by the educational climate* in which it takes place: the settings and surroundings, the influences of others, and the values accorded to the life of the mind and to learning achievements.

   The *educational climates* in which learning occurs best:
   - value academic and personal success and intellectual inquiry;
   - involve **all constituents**—faculty, students, staff, alumni, employers, family, and others—in **contributing** to student learning;
   - make student learning and development an integral part of **faculty and staff responsibilities and rewards**;
   - incorporate student **academic performance and development goals** into the educational mission, and assessment of progress toward them into unit performance.
   - include subcommunities in which students feel connected, cared for, and trusted.

To construct an effective educational climate, faculty and staff collaborators:

- build a strong sense of community among all institutional constituencies;
- organize ceremonies to honor and highlight contributions to community life and educational values;
- publicly celebrate institutional values;
- articulate how each administrative and academic unit serves the institution's mission; and
- share and use information on how units are performing in relation to this mission.

The Youth in Transition Program of *James Madison University* (Virginia) introduces academically underprepared minority students to college life beginning in the summer prior to their freshman year. Students are supported by an intensive, **nurturing educational environment** in which they can overcome prior negative learning experiences and develop new ways to succeed in academics. The program, offered jointly by university faculty and the Office of Multicultural Student Services, continues throughout the school year. Students receive ongoing academic support, educational enrichment opportunities, and mentors. Academic progress is monitored continuously. Faculty and student affairs staff work as an instructional team, with faculty teaching basic mathematics and writing skills and staff teaching study skills and time management and addressing issues of independence and self-confidence. Students live together in residence halls to establish peer relationships and work with their advisors through all four years of college.

A study of program participants tracked their academic progress over a one-year period. Results showed an increase in the proportion of minority students in good standing over the course of the year and a decrease in the number placed on suspension. Further analysis indicated that a significant proportion of those placed on suspension were later able to return to good standing.

New Century College of *George Mason University* (Virginia) coordinates Collaborations: Partnerships for Active Communities, a combination of programs designed to **place students in diverse educational settings**. "Adventure learning" courses, which fulfill the college's requirement for experiential learning, include the Chesapeake Bay Program and the Bahamas Environmental Research Center, where students engage the natural environment firsthand and learn about ecology in the broadest sense, including the people and cultures that shape the environment. Courses contain both a classroom component and a co-curricular final project. Students also can enroll in skill-based short courses, in learning communities that connect classroom study with life experiences, or in an alternative spring break through which they contribute to and learn about communities they serve. Students are encouraged to reflect on their experiences by developing portfolios representative of their work, providing documentation of work in progress, and presenting evidence of self-reflection on how their learning experiences have evolved.

Comparisons show that students who have participated in these programs have higher retention rates, academic performance, and satisfaction with college life than do non-participants.

7. Learning requires *frequent feedback* if it is to be sustained, *practice* if it is to be nourished, and *opportunities to use* what has been learned.

The importance to learning of *feedback, practice, and use* of knowledge and skills mandates that students be:

- expected to **meet high but achievable standards** and provided timely information on their progress toward meeting them;
- engaged in a recurring process of **correction and improvement**;
- encouraged to **take risks** and **learn from mistakes**;
- taught how to be **constructive critics** of each other's work;
- required to demonstrate their learning accomplishments through **active problem solving, applying concepts** to practical situations;
- **refining skills** through frequent use; and
- asked to test theory against practice and refine theory based on practice.

To provide occasions to use and practice what has been learned, faculty and staff collaborators:

- recruit students with relevant academic interests as active participants and leaders in related campus life programs and activities;
- organize work opportunities to take advantage of students' developing skills and knowledge;
- collaborate with businesses and community organizations to match students to internship and externship experiences that fit their evolving educational profiles; and
- develop student research and design projects based on actual problems or cases presented by external organizations to be resolved.

Iowa State University's College of Design and Department of Residence have created together the Design Exchange, a living and learning experience to promote academic success. The Exchange houses design students together in a learning community that includes a design studio and computer laboratory. The studio is available twenty-four hours a day and serves as the site of biweekly sessions ranging from academic survival skills to portfolio development. Sessions are facilitated by faculty, student affairs, and residence assistance staff; upper-class design students serve as peer mentors and advisors, role models, and programmers. Efforts are made to offer out-of-class activities that extend classroom learning, and to encourage informal interaction among faculty, staff, and students. First-semester survival programs are followed by more intentional faculty involvement in the second semester, during which they discuss with students such issues as design portfolios and career development. The program allows students to **create design projects and receive continual feedback** from peers and teachers. The studio space encourages this sharing on a cooperative rather than a competitive basis.

Preliminary data from a study comparing Exchange students with a control group suggest that students enrolled in the program have higher grade-point averages than design students not involved in the learning community. Students in the program also report higher levels of satisfaction with the university, a greater sense of community, and improved ability to work collaboratively to find solutions to curricular and social issues. Students surveyed cite frequent feedback and living together as major benefits of the program.

The undergraduate division of the Wharton School of the *University of Pennsylvania* has a mission to educate students to become broad-minded, articulate, and effective leaders in the global marketplace. Its course on leadership and communication in groups is a collaboration between student and academic affairs designed to serve this mission. It features community service projects that provide opportunities to **develop and refine leadership skills** both inside and outside the classroom. Other cooperative experiential activities over the course of students' four-year experience include leadership retreats, mentoring programs, skill-building workshops, a leadership lecture series, the management of forty student clubs and organizations, and student-run conferences. The academic and student service partnership is supported by team advisors, trained to offer both academic advice and peer counseling. The collaboration also works to temper the highly competitive business school culture and to foster cooperative community and college leaders.

Student surveys show appreciation for the school's ability to meet their needs for leadership skills. Students evaluate the leadership retreats highly. In addition, students from the school serve an already large and increasing proportion of leadership positions in the university's student organizations.

8. Much learning *takes place informally and incidentally,* beyond explicit teaching or the classroom, in casual contacts with faculty and staff, peers, campus life, active social and community involvements, and unplanned but fertile and complex situations.

Informal and incidental learning is enhanced by:
- activities beyond the classroom that enrich formal learning experiences;
- an institutional climate that encourages student interaction related to educational issues;
- mentorship relationships on and off campus;
- chances for students to meet faculty and staff in a variety of settings and circumstances; and
- student participation as volunteers and active citizens in the broader community.

To facilitate informal and incidental learning, faculty and staff collaborators:
- sponsor programs for students, faculty, and staff that serve both social and educational purposes;

- organize community service and service-learning activities performed by faculty, staff, and students together;
- design campus life programs that relate directly to specific courses;
- link students with peers and with faculty, staff, and community mentors; and
- build common gathering places for students, faculty, and staff.

The First-Year Program at the *College of the Holy Cross* (Massachusetts) is a thematically based academic experience for about one-fourth of the first-year class. Each year a new theme is built around the question "How then shall we live?" by connecting that question to a specific issue. The theme gives an explicit ethical focus to the year and is the touchstone for all other components of the program, including a pair of first-year courses extending through both semesters, a two-semester common reading program, a variety of co-curricular events with faculty and students, and a common residency experience. The intellectual community associated with the program encompasses classroom, studio, laboratory, performance space, faculty offices, and residence hall. The program extends into all aspects of students' lives, connecting the learning experience with fundamental questions about how to live, to be part of a community, and to make moral choices. The intent is to provide shared experiences that embrace the entire first-year environment and in so doing to provide a framework that promotes informal learning.

Student interviews and institutional records show high levels of participation in class discussion and co-curricular events, extensive discussions outside the classroom, and a strong sense of community in the residence halls. Compared with other students, First-Year participants had fewer alcohol-related incidents, received higher grades, and were more likely to assume campus leadership positions, to participate in honors and study abroad programs, and to be active in community programs.

The *University of Missouri, Columbia* creates Freshmen Interest Groups of students enrolled in the same sections of three general education courses, living in the same residence halls (usually on the same floor), and enrolled in a one-semester seminar. The seminar is designed to help students integrate material from the general education courses and to facilitate informal discussions on issues covered in the courses. The program's objectives are to make the campus psychologically small by creating peer reference groups of students, to integrate purposefully curricular and co-curricular experiences, to stimulate early registration for related courses, and to encourage faculty to integrate course content and activities across their disciplines. Faculty and staff jointly plan the program, coordinate in- and out-of-classroom activities, and champion desired outcomes and assessment strategies to evaluate the impact of the learning experience. Shared projects and events associated with the courses are especially important for promoting opportunities for discussion. Peer advisors reinforce this learning, serve as study leaders, and use team-building approaches to increase interest group cohesion. Residence halls have been renovated to offer group study space, classrooms, and computer laboratories.

In comparison with other freshmen, students in the Freshmen Interest Groups demonstrate higher levels of interaction and involvement in college life in the first and second years, greater intellectual content in their contacts with faculty and other students, better performance in general education courses, higher grade-point averages, and higher freshmen-to-sophomore retention rates.

9. Learning is *grounded in particular contexts and individual experiences,* requiring effort to transfer specific knowledge and skills to other circumstances or to more general understandings and to unlearn personal views and approaches when confronted by new information.

The *grounded* nature of learning requires that students:
- encounter alternative perspectives and others' realities;
- grapple with educational materials that challenge conventional views;
- confront novel circumstances that extend beyond their own personal experiences and that require the application of new knowledge or more general principles; and
- share freely with others experiences that have shaped their identities.

To transform learning *grounded in particular contexts and individual experiences* into broader understandings, faculty and staff collaborators:
- sponsor events that involve students with new people and situations;
- champion occasions for interdisciplinary discourse on salient issues;
- foster dialogues between people with disparate perspectives and backgrounds; and
- expand study abroad and cultural exchange programs.

St. Lawrence University (New York) strives for a learning environment that integrates multicultural perspectives, influences, and ideas throughout the curriculum and the campus community. In its First-Year Program, students live together in residential colleges and take an intensive, year-long, interdisciplinary, team-taught thematic course in communication. Faculty members work with student affairs staff to ensure that the living and learning nature of the program encourages students to reflect on course themes, conflicts arising in the residence hall, and connections between the themes and living experiences. A "residential curriculum" is organized by residential coordinators, college assistants, and faculty to discuss in class and in the colleges both predictable and unique stresses in the residence communities. A residential education committee plans events and designs interventions to address student problems and conflicts. Students are expected to think through and resolve conflicts associated with differences in background, in behavior within the residence halls, and in academic perspectives. In doing so, students explore each other's personal histories, respond to others' views, and examine the relationship between individual perspectives and knowledge-based approaches.

Detailed evaluation forms ask students about the impact of living with people enrolled in a common course, the communication and research skills learned, the effects of the multidisciplinary, team-taught course, and the coverage of residential issues. Data indicate that residential goals and communications skills are being achieved. Students are positive about living with others who share their academic and personal experiences and appreciate having faculty involved in their residential lives.

University of Wisconsin, Whitewater has a mission to serve students with disabilities and has had a formal program to provide services for these students for nearly thirty years. Instructional staff accommodate students with disabilities in classrooms, labs, field work, internships, student teaching, and the workplace. A new work experience project offering academic credit has received exceptional support from faculty and students. The project brings staff into close contact with faculty, and staff work with the State Vocational Rehabilitation Agency to organize the experience. For many severely and multiply disabled students, the work is one of the first successful validations of their capacity to succeed and to establish a strong identity. Efforts are focused on matching students' needs with a work environment complementing their educational background and likely to ensure success. The work is an intensive individual experience; however, the individual learning is tied directly to interaction with others in the workplace at several levels. It helps to provide self-definition as a person and to delineate a role and status within the task group. The combination of the workplace routine, supervisory and peer feedback, and the duties of the position offer opportunities for growth and for eliminating non-functional behaviors. The program has proved particularly important for individuals whose learning styles are not conducive to transfer of knowledge from one context to another.

At the university, students with disabilities are retained at a significantly higher rate than the institutional average for all students, and they obtain employment at exceptional rates. These results compare remarkably well with national studies of retention and employment rates for disabled students.

Bowling Green State University (Ohio) created its Chapman Learning Center as a "think tank for learning," to experiment with new pedagogies and program structures to engage students in classroom and outside-the-classroom activities. A freshmen residential program, the Center involves faculty from several disciplines, each with offices in the residence hall, a hall director and junior tutors who work with faculty on required anchor courses, elective courses, and a common learning day. Classes are thematically linked in two anchor courses each semester, and center on difficult social issues during the first term and on aesthetics and imagination during the second. Freshmen composition courses are linked to these disciplinary courses. Community events are planned to relate directly to the course themes. Teaching practices emphasize interactive, experiential activities, learning experiences outside the classroom, critical thinking about challenging issues, and support for learning by residential staff. Classes are small, to enable faculty to offer frequent written and verbal feedback on in-class and out-of-class assignments. Students are encouraged to examine personal beliefs and values in relation to broader perspectives on social issues, and peer-mediated discussions of social controversies are featured.

Chapman students show disproportionate satisfaction and adjustment to college life when compared with other freshmen. They feel less lonely, are more actively involved in their classes, experience more faculty approval, and are more willing to approach faculty.

10. Learning involves *the ability of individuals to monitor their own learning,* to understand how knowledge is acquired, to develop strategies for learning based on discerning their capacities and limitations, and to be aware of their own ways of knowing in approaching new bodies of knowledge and disciplinary frameworks.

To improve the ability of individuals to *monitor* their *own learning* requires that faculty and staff:
- assist students in understanding the elements and structures of learning and the standards for learning achievements;
- help students understand their relative strengths and weaknesses in learning;
- ask students to observe and record their own progress in learning;
- use multiple pedagogies suited to the content or skills to be learned and reaching students with different approaches to learning;
- tailor education to the individual learner rather than exclusively providing mass-delivered presentations;
- use educational technologies as a tool for collaborative learning and encourage reticent students to participate;
- cultivate students' desire to know what they do not know; and
- continue to learn what factors affect student cognition and learning and to design learning experiences responsive to learning differences.

To enable students to monitor their own learning, faculty and staff collaborators:
- help them delineate and articulate their learning interests, strengths, and deficiencies;
- reduce the risk to students of acknowledging their own limitations;
- help students select curricular and other educational experiences covering a broad range of learning approaches and performance evaluations; and
- create faculty and staff development activities to learn about advances in learning theory and practice.

The Western College Program of *Miami University, Oxford* (Ohio) is an interdisciplinary residential college featuring a core curriculum in the liberal arts for students' first two years. In their junior year, students are provided opportunities to take greater responsibility for and to monitor, their

learning through individually designed upper-level interdisciplinary programs of study and a year-long senior project based on all four years of
study. Completed senior projects are publicly presented using a professional
conference format and including faculty respondents from outside the college who have not worked with the students. Faculty and student affairs
staff collaborate to fuse the living and study experience and to challenge and
support students as they pursue their core and self-designed studies.

The Student Affairs Assessment Committee, comprised of student, academic and business affairs staff, documents the impact that the university
is having on students inside and outside the classroom. Measures include
quantitative, nationally normed outcome assessment instruments and qualitative evaluations based on student interviews, free writing, focus groups,
portfolios of student work, and ethnographies.

The vice presidents for academic and student affairs at *William Rainey
Harper College* (Illinois) established a joint "Statement of Student Success"
that endorses two concepts: all students have the right to succeed, and the
college has the right to uphold high standards for achievement. Based on this
statement, the college established a program to support students at this two-
year open-door college with academic preparation and counseling services
as a way to meet the college's standards and to help them attain success. The
college developed five standards of academic performance, established
requirements for entry into college-level courses based on level of preparation as determined by entrance tests, and coupled these actions with an
"intrusive intervention" program administered by the student development
office. The intervention program monitors student course taking and grades.
Through computerized tracking and human interaction, students receive
information on their progress and work with faculty and staff to create personalized success contracts. These contracts include academic, personal,
developmental, and social strategies to assist students making decisions
about college and careers. Individual students' strategies are recorded and
tracked through a computerized interface with the registration system, allowing possible restrictions to course loads or future registrations, or triggering
further interventions when performance falls below standards. Interventions
are made by faculty and staff, and students are asked to assess their own performance and to learn ways to use the support system to assist them.

Survey results over the years document that at-risk students enrolled
in the intervention program have a clear understanding of the academic system, know what factors result in low grades, have reasonable plans to
improve their performance, and believe the required interventions will have
a positive impact on their future academic success.

What We Have Learned

Collaborative Futures in Support of Learning. The evolving principles of learning, continually informed by future advances in our understanding and knowledge of the learning process, hold great promise for

improved student learning. By applying these principles to the practice of teaching, the development of curricula, the design of learning environments, and the assessment of learning, we will achieve more powerful learning. Realizing the full benefit of these applications depends upon collaborative efforts between academic and student affairs professionals—and beyond. It will require attention and action by all those affiliated with our institutions as well as by members of the larger community concerned with higher education to ensure that we achieve our mission of increased higher learning.

We call all those who serve the goals of learning to contribute to these collaborations. We ask that:

Students take charge of their own learning and organize their educational programs to include a broad array of experiences both inside and outside the classroom; become aware of the cumulative nature of their education, and consequently plan and monitor their development; and establish personal relationships with faculty and staff as an essential part of their education.

Faculty become masters of cognitive studies; develop pedagogy and curricula that draw upon and embody learning principles; become involved in all aspects of their institution's community life; and work in partnership with staff and community supporters to create learning activities based on the learning principles.

Scholars of cognition share their findings widely with faculty colleagues and higher education audiences and be attentive in their writings to the application of new findings to the conduct of teaching and learning.

Administrative leaders rethink the conventional organization of colleges and universities to create more inventive structures and processes that integrate academic and student affairs; align institutional planning, hiring, rewards, and resource allocations with the learning mission; offer professional development opportunities for people to cooperate across institutional boundaries; use evidence of student learning to guide program improvement, planning and resource allocation; and communicate information on students' life circumstances and culture to all members of the college or university community.

Student affairs professionals and other staff take the initiative to connect to each other and to academic units; develop programs that purposefully incorporate and identify learning contributions; and help students to view their education holistically and to participate fully in the life of the institution and the community.

Alumni reflect upon how what they learned in college contributed to their life after graduation and share these observations with current students and institutional officials; provide learning opportunities and mentorships outside the classroom for students; and contribute financial support to programs offering students the chance to use their knowledge in a variety of settings.

Governing boards understand the learning enterprise and how the institution conducts it; ask senior managers for information on how the organizational structure supports learning and for evidence of learning outcomes; and reward contributions to learning through promotion and tenure decisions and in evaluation of the president.

Community supporters volunteer workplace and other organizational venues for student learning; team with faculty and staff to design learning experiences in the community or workplace; serve as supervisors and mentors for student learning activities; evaluate student performance and provide models of reflective practice in their own professions; and help colleges and universities to understand the skills and knowledge needed by their graduates.

Accrediting agencies require in their review processes evidence of how institutions integrate learning experiences across administrative units and demand measures of learning effectiveness.

Professional associations disseminate best practices of collaboration on behalf of student learning in their programs, publications, and awards; exemplify the importance of partnerships for learning by establishing cooperative programs with other associations; and emphasize learning as a field of knowledge essential for graduate students planning careers in colleges or universities.

Families help students select a college or university based on its commitments to learning and student development and its learning environment; encourage students to choose and participate in a comprehensive program of educational activities throughout their collegiate experience; and help students to understand the value of reflection and to find time for concentrated study in their complicated lives.

Government agencies sponsor research and development on learning; offer incentives to institutions for new initiatives focused on collaboration for learning; and require evidence of institutional assessment of learning.

All those involved in higher education, as professionals or as community supporters, view themselves as teachers, learners, and collaborators in service to learning.

Joint Task Force Members

Judith Berson
Associate Vice President for Student
   Affairs
Broward Community College

Susan Engelkemeyer
Professor
Babson College

Paul M. Oliaro
Vice President for Student Affairs
West Chester University of Pennsylvania

David L. Potter (*chair*)
Provost
George Mason University

Patrick T. Terenzini
Professor and Senior Scientist
Center on the Study of Higher Education
The Pennsylvania State University

Geneva M. Walker-Johnson
Dean of Student Life
Hartwick College

The Joint Task Force on Student Learning gratefully acknowledges the contributions
   of the following:

Association Representatives

President
Margaret A. Miller
American Association for Higher
   Education (AAHE)

Lynn Willett
President, American College Personnnel
   Association (ACPA), and Vice
   President, Student Affairs, Bridgewater
   State College

Jack Warner
National Association of Student
   Personnel Administrators (NASPA) and
   Vice Chancellor, Massachusetts Board
   of Higher Education

Contact
Barbara Cambridge
Director, AAHE Teaching Initiatives,
   AAHE

Carmen Neuberger
Executive Director, ACPA

Gwendolyn Dungy
Executive Director, NASPA

Task Force Support
Scott Brown
Doctoral Intern, AAHE

Resource Group

K. Patricia Cross
David Pierpont Gardner
Professor of Higher Education
University of California-Berkeley

Jon C. Dalton
Vice President for Student Affairs
Florida State University

Dean L. Hubbard
President
Northwest Missouri State University

George Kuh
Professor of Education
Indiana University Bloomington

Theodore J. Marchese
Vice President
AAHE

Shelia Murphy
Dean of Student Life
Simmons College

Dennis Roberts
Assistant Vice President for Student
   Affairs
Miami University

William L. Thomas, Jr.
Vice President for Student Affairs
University of Maryland, College Park

2

Colleges and universities have different reasons for collaborative efforts, different problems with them, and different solutions.

Documenting the Landscape: Results of a National Study on Academic and Student Affairs Collaborations

Adrianna Kezar

For the past decade, national student affairs associations and several higher education scholars have been advocating academic and student affairs collaborations. The National Association of Student Personnel Administrators (NASPA) suggests as part of its *Principles of Good Practice for Student Affairs* (1997) that administrators forge educational partnerships that advance student learning. Likewise, the American College Personnel Association (ACPA) has listed "Collaboration and Partnerships" as a major trend for the twenty-first century (1999). In a combined effort, the American Association for Higher Education (AAHE), ACPA, and NASPA published the report *Powerful Partnerships: A Shared Responsibility for Learning* (1998). This report contains principles for collaboration and provides examples of institutions that have found success through partnerships between academic and student affairs.

Despite these and other calls for student and academic affairs collaborations, as well as some examples of successful practices and principles, almost no empirical research exists regarding the extent to which this practice is currently taking place. Furthermore, researchers have not identified the most successful types of collaboration, the reasons people collaborate, strategies for creating collaborations, or the characteristics of successful collaborations. In response to this need for empirical data, the Educational Resources Information Center Clearinghouse on Higher Education, NASPA, and ACPA joined forces to conduct a national study of academic and student affairs collaborations. This chapter reviews the results of this national research project, presenting a picture of the type of collaborations that currently exist and institutional experiences with these partnerships.

NEW DIRECTIONS FOR HIGHER EDUCATION, no. 116, Winter 2001 © Wiley Periodicals, Inc.

The Study: Academic and Student Affairs Collaboration

Because the study endeavored to provide a national picture of trends related to academic and student affairs collaboration, survey methodology was chosen. This approach allowed the research team to discover trends among different institution types, sizes, types of student, campus cultures, and structures that were assumed to impact the extent and success of collaborations. The survey examined the following areas: (1) student affairs involvement in institutional-level decision making, (2) the reasons for collaboration, (3) the types of collaboration that exist, (4) what made these collaborations successful, (5) what new structures or models were used to facilitate collaboration, (6) what strategies were most successful, (7) obstacles for collaboration, (8) outcomes assessment of collaboration efforts, and (9) institutional characteristics. The team chose these concepts and issues based on the student affairs literature related to academic and student affairs collaboration and organizational literature on cross-divisional teams and change.

The survey was next reviewed by the ACPA and NASPA senior scholars and pilot tested among twenty administrators on college campuses. After comments were incorporated from the pilot test, the survey was loaded on a Web site (in May 2000) and a letter sent out to survey participants, with a link to the survey. Two follow-up notices were sent in July and August encouraging participation.

Chief student affairs officers were chosen as the sample for the survey because they would most likely have the most accurate and thorough knowledge about collaborations among academic and student affairs on campuses. The total population is approximately thirty-five hundred individuals. A sample of 260 individuals was chosen for the study and was made representative to the overall population based on institutional type and characteristics. Of these, 128 individuals returned the survey for a survey response of 49 percent.

Survey responses were directly downloaded from an ACCESS database into statistical database SPSS. Frequencies were run for each variable, and cross tabulations were run among variables to identify relationships. Possible relationships were tested for significance using Pearson chi-square tests. Some variables were recoded to collapse categories with few responses. For example, vocational and technical colleges were combined with community colleges. Factors were developed among subquestions addressing similar concepts such as reasons for collaboration; all reasons related to learning were combined.

This study has several limitations. First, the response rate was only 49 percent. Although that is an acceptable rate for conducting analysis and making generalizations, claims must be made with caution because half of those surveyed did not respond. Furthermore, due to the low number of survey responses, statistical significance may not emerge, even though there may be a relationship in a larger sample size. In addition, because one type of collaboration was not examined across the entire survey, the researchers were unable to run analysis by cases for individual types of collaborations (e.g., academic advising vs. learning communities). Although some statements can be made about these more specific collaborations, they must be made carefully.

The National Landscape: Growing Collaboration and Emerging Strategies for Institutionalization

Every institution surveyed was engaged in some form of collaboration between academic and student affairs. A large portion of institutions have three to five moderately or very successful collaborations, approximately 50 institutions that responded to the survey, or 40 percent. In addition, 30 percent have six or more campus collaborations that are moderately or very successful. Although this signals a fairly high level of success for 70 percent of the institutions, 30 percent had zero to two moderately or very successful collaborations. As a national picture, this presents quite a promising picture. The message about the importance of student and academic affairs collaboration appears to have reached campuses, and they are trying to meaningfully engage in collaborations. Many are experiencing high levels of success among a set of collaborations, but the data also help us to understand where successes and challenges exist.

What types of activities or programs are most successful? Overwhelming, institutions are experiencing the most success with counseling, first-year experience programs, orientation, and recruitment. Perhaps institutions perceive that the first year is an area in which collaboration is particularly critical. Regardless of the reason, the success of first-year programs provides change agents with ideas for where to begin collaboration efforts if they have been unsuccessful or not engaged in collaboration. After first-year programs, institutions appear to have the most success with cocurricular activities.

In general, institutions were moderately successful with academic advising, community-service learning, diversity programs, leadership development, retention plans, and student conduct. The common ground for this set of activities is that they are mostly cocurricular. Historically, leadership training or academic advising has been offered jointly by academic and student affairs. Institutions can build on these areas of common interest to develop seamless programs. The least-successful collaborations occurred among faculty development, senior-year experience, and self-design or independent course work. Perhaps these are areas that have traditionally been part of academic affairs. Nonetheless, the fewest number of institutions had attempted these collaborations.

Another important lesson from the study is that collaboration in and of itself is useful. There is a statistically significant relationship between success in one form of collaboration (cocurricular or curricular) and success in the other. Therefore, it seems useful to start in areas where institutions are experiencing the most success (e.g., counseling, first-year experience, orientation, recruitment) and to build from there; once an institution is successful with one form of collaboration (cocurricular or curricular), it tends to be successful in the other. Efforts to build collaboration in any area seem to help create success for collaboration in other programs. Are there variations by institutional type? There were a few statistically significant differences. For example, institutions with enrollments of ten thousand and above were more likely to be successful with curricular collaborations. Public four-year and comprehensive institutions were the most successful with partnerships, with over 54 percent having six or more successful collaborations compared with 27 percent at private schools and 18 percent at community colleges. Institutions with predominantly full-time students were slightly more likely to have more successful collaborations than those with greater numbers of part-time students.

Many institutional characteristics were not statistically significant, and others I was unable to test due to low cell count (insufficient amount of data). Yet there were certain trends in the data. There is a slight relationship between funding and number of successful collaborations—with six or more successful collaborations, there is a trend for increasing funds that appears to be even more strongly related to curricular collaborations. Also, the institutions identified themselves as having three predominant cultures: growing demands, research as a priority, and learning as a priority. There was a trend for more success among collaborations on campuses with cultures of growing demands. What does this all mean? Funding may facilitate the possibility for partnerships, growing demands may actually help provide impetus for people to focus on working together, and community colleges and institutions with a part-time student body may experience greater difficulty.

Institutional type was related to areas of differential success among programs. Community colleges excelled in academic advising, academic integrity, career development, counseling, diversity, and faculty development. It is probably not surprising that community colleges are better able to collaborate on certain academic issues that private four-year and comprehensive institutions find difficult because faculty at the community colleges neither have the same disciplinary affiliation nor expertise in individually designing curriculum and learning experiences. Public four-year and comprehensive institutions, on the other hand, experienced the most success with assessment of learning, athletics, community service, diversity, financial aid, and first-year experience. These institutions are excelling in areas in which student affairs has traditionally been involved; thus, they are building on areas of their expertise and bringing faculty into the partnership. Private four-year institutions were strongest with athletics, community service, community standards, and first-year experience. These institutions also followed the trend for public four-year and comprehensive institutions of having success among cocurricular areas.

Why Institutions Are Engaging in Partnerships

The survey examined four primary reasons—learning as a priority, collegial environment, managerial/accountability, and new leadership/leadership philosophy—that institutions might engage in collaborations between academic and student affairs and tried to determine if reasons for engaging in collaboration related to success. Because partnerships have been shown to enhance student learning, it seemed important to determine if learning was a primary reason for collaborations. Collegial environment investigates whether the campus has a tradition, ethic, or philosophy that encourages collaboration. Managerial or accountability refers to pressures from state legislatures, accreditors, boards, or internal administrators to partner to enhance learning and demonstrate positive outcomes for students. And new leadership/leadership belief refers to people on campus with authority encouraging collaboration.

Learning (35 percent) was by far the most important reason for engaging in collaboration, followed by leadership (27 percent) and collegiality (22 percent). Managerial and accountability (16 percent) were mentioned less often, but the student-as-customer (9 percent) did emerge as an oft-cited reason among many institutions. In terms of learning, retention and keeping student learning as a focus were noted most often whereas for leadership, the reason was usually new leadership on campus. In response to creating a collegial environment, a history of collaboration and collegial campus culture was the reason most often cited for engaging in collaboration. Reasons varied by institutional type, with community colleges (43 percent) and public four-year institutions (43 percent) more likely to describe leadership and private four-year institutions more likely to cite learning (49 percent) followed by collegiality (42 percent).

Did the institutions' reasons for engaging in collaboration impact their number of successful collaborations or ability to succeed? Yes and no. Institutions that emphasized student learning were slightly more successful with cocurricular collaborations. However, those with three to five and six or more successful curricular collaborations were more likely to have cited collegiality or leadership as significant reasons. Although this relationship was not statistically significant (based on too many choices of reasons; cell size was too small), it appears that institutions that are interested in shifting from non- or cocurricular collaborations to curricular collaborations may want to look at their underlying philosophies or reasons for doing so. Although it seems counterintuitive that a focus on learning would not be associated with more success on curricular collaborations, it may be that building an environment of collegiality is key. Further study of this finding is needed.

Engaging in Collaboration: Strategies and Facilitators

The research team investigated both institutional perceptions about what made collaborations successful and strategies used. Each of these areas was also examined in relation to the actual number of successful collaborations; this second analysis provided a way to move beyond perceptions to identify what was actually related to successful partnerships. The team overwhelmingly found that cooperation (73 percent), student affairs staff attitudes (66 percent), common goals (63 percent), and personalities (62 percent) were believed to make the most difference in the success of collaborative efforts. In open-ended responses, most people mentioned that new people had come to campus or that there was new leadership, which helped significantly in making the change. New people were not a choice on the survey, so this factor may be underestimated in importance.

The findings about the importance of individuals contradicts most of the recent literature about change and collaboration, which identifies structural changes, planning, and senior administrative support or leadership as significant to creating working partnerships. For example, student affairs officers cited additional resources as most important only 17 percent, incentives 8 percent, redefining mission 15 percent, and change in job responsibilities 20 percent. These strategies (incentives, realigning budgets, and restructuring) are among some of the key levers in the change literature. In fact, 65 percent of respondents stated that what was termed in the study human or cultural characteristics best defined reasons for success in academic and student affairs, whereas structural variables were only most important in approximately 25 percent of the responses. Perhaps the human-development orientation or culture of student affairs makes these professionals more likely to assign institutional change to individual interactions and issues rather than institutional changes or approaches.

It is critical to look at this finding in relation to the strategies that were actually associated with successful collaborations. Responses to actual strategies that were related to successful collaboration differed from perceived strategies. In examining what student affairs officers thought were the most successful strategies for creating change, a combination of human-oriented (39 percent noted as most successful of overall cultural responses), structural (23 percent noted as most successful of overall structural responses), and senior administrative support (80 percent noted this as very successful, separated out from other two because this was the most often cited strategy for success) strategies were noted as necessary for creating change. In terms of human-oriented strategies, the researchers combined several of the individual survey responses for analysis: cross-institutional dialogue, common language development, common vision, generating enthusiasm, marketing change, and staff development. In terms of structural approaches, researchers created a new variable with consultants, combining fiscal resources, systemic orientation, incentives (monetary and nonmonetary), planning, change in promotion and tenure requirements, restructuring, reward system altered, and setting expectations and accountability. Student affairs officers reported that they used cultural approaches more often than structural strategies (64 percent of total cases used more than three structural strategies, whereas 98 percent used more than three cultural strategies).

Finally, senior administrative support was made a separate strategy because it is an aspect of both cultural and structural approaches to change; within cultural approaches, it is more often referred to as leadership. It is important to note that senior administrative support was by far the most often cited variable for success, with 80 percent stating that it was a very successful strategy for creating partnerships between academic and student affairs. There was a statistically significant variance by institutional type, with public four-year and comprehensive institutions citing senior administrative support as less important than private four-year and community colleges. Other data support this finding of the lesser importance of leadership at four-year public and comprehensive institutions, for example, the statistically significant relationship among structural strategies such as additional resources and incentives. At larger institutions, resources and incentives were needed for establishing institutional priorities, whereas on small campuses, this could often be accomplished through the leader describing priorities.

The importance of leadership needed further analysis because respondents to surveys often overinflate the importance of senior administrative support or leadership. Thus, this finding was tested for statistical significance against the number of successful collaborations that actually occurred. It was not found to be significant, meaning that it was less important than people estimated. There needs to be more investigation into the role of senior administrative support, but clearly people felt it was important on their campuses. In open-ended responses about strategies, it was noted that senior administrative support was key to accessing resources for collaboration, hiring new staff aligned with the philosophy, and signaling institutional priority. There may be some colinearity or overlap between strategies related to incentives or restructuring and senior administrative support. Perhaps senior administrative support is seen as a way to access resources necessary for incentives or restructuring, making it significant in respondent's perception.

Analysis showed a statistically significant relationship between structural strategies and the number of successful collaborations. The more structural strategies used, the greater the number of successful collaborations. Unfortunately, it was impossible to test the relationship of cultural strategies to successful number of collaborations because all respondents used cultural strategies; there was no variation in usage. However, from the descriptive statistics, it is clear that the more cultural strategies used, the more number of successful collaborations. Thus, it appears that both structural and cultural strategies are critical for creating changes on campus. More detail about the individual responses will help to illustrate this pattern.

Of the individual strategies, a combination of cultural and structural strategies was found critical for developing change: leadership (80 percent very successful; 98 percent of respondents answered very or moderately successful) was far and above the most important individual strategy, followed by cross-institutional dialogue (57 percent very successful; 93 percent of respondents answered very or moderately successful), setting expectations (44 percent very successful; 93 percent of respondents answered very or moderately successful), generating enthusiasm (41 percent very successful; 94 percent of respondents answered very or moderately successful), creating a common vision (39 percent very successful; 93 percent of respondents answered very or moderately successful), staff development (40 percent very successful; 89 percent of respondents answered very or moderately successful), and planning (30 percent very successful; 90 percent of respondents answered very or moderately successful).

Because student affairs staff underestimate the value of setting expectations (93 percent very or moderately successful), planning (90 percent very or moderately successful), systemic change (78 percent very or moderately successful), restructuring (66 percent very or moderately successful), combining fiscal resources (63 percent very or moderately successful), and incentives (53 percent very or moderately successful), they may not use these strategies that appear to be related to numbers of successful collaborations. The open-ended responses to the survey about successful strategies also reinforce the importance of structural approaches. Several individuals mentioned that they had developed an enrollment management division that structurally connects academic and student affairs, cross-unit teams that involve all staff in planning, dual admissions processes, incorporation of business process reengineering, mapping collaborations, and the development of learning communities. These new joint structures were also reinforced by another part of the survey that examined structural changes. Although many institutions have not engaged in restructuring, those that did cited joint council or committees (86 percent very and moderately successful), learning communities (74 percent very and moderately successful), change in student affairs job (70 percent very and moderately successful), and redesign of physical space (70 percent very and moderately successful) as significant to their ability to create collaboration. This is not to say that cultural approaches were not the most successful strategies overall, but many of the individual structural strategies were statistically significant in relationship to creating successful collaborations and tend to be underestimated by student affairs staff.

Because all institutions are not alike, it is important to examine institutional characteristics to determine if there are variations. Surprisingly, there were few statistical relationships between institutional characteristics and success with using cultural or structural strategies. Both strategies appear to be important at all institution types. However, public four-year institutions were more likely to use the array of structural strategies than community colleges or private four-year institutions. This finding may reflect the fact that larger institutions feel the need to use incentives, restructuring, and other strategies that help to overcome institutional size.

Although I will discuss a few other trends in the data, none of these emerged as statistically significant. Senior administrative support, for example, is slightly more important in institutions with an enrollment of three thousand or less. This may be because leaders in smaller environments have a greater ability to be influential. At institutions with enrollments of ten thousand or more students, structural strategies and strategies that involve money or incentives are slightly more important. These two findings are supported by the literature on institutional change; larger organizations tend to need more alterations to the structure, particularly incentives, because it is too difficult to alter the entire culture or reach the whole community. Type of students (mostly full-time, mostly part-time, or half-and-half) and level of funding did not appear related to success among partnerships. Organizational structure of academic and student affairs also does not appear to be related, but there were too few people in the survey that had totally or partially combined their operations to conduct analysis.

What Stands in the Way? Obstacles and Barriers to Change

The research team felt it important to understand obstacles that institutions face. The literature on change in higher education suggests that an important part of preparing an institution for a change is identifying obstacles (Kezar, 2001). The most often cited obstacles were lack of faculty and staff time (35 percent significant; 82 percent very and moderate obstacle), faculty disciplinary ties (34 percent significant; 75 percent very and moderate obstacle), faculty resistance (39 percent significant; 72 percent very and moderate obstacle), and lack of established goals (21 percent very; 63 percent very and moderate obstacle). Interestingly, senior administrative support, the most important facilitator of change, was only a modest barrier if it was missing (20 percent significant; 35 percent significant and modest). This again suggests that individuals in the survey may have overemphasized this element.

Similar to the responses concerning perceptions about what makes collaborations successful, chief student affairs officers identified more human- or cultural-oriented obstacles. Examination of the relationship of obstacles with types of changes (particular programs) showed that more obstacles appeared to be related to curricular collaborations, but the difference was not statistically significant. Overall, there are more structural obstacles noted by respondents, but the three most often cited obstacles were cultural.

A small number of trends in the data related to differences among institutional type, but few of these differences were statistically significant. There was a statistically significant relationship between institutional type and number of structural obstacles, with 68 percent of public four-year and comprehensive institutions experiencing three or more structural obstacles. Community colleges actually noted the fewest structural obstacles. This result may be based on the reduced priority of research and disciplinary societies to divide faculty time, reward structures, tenure, and other boundaries that separate academic and student affairs and impact faculty time and motivation. There were slightly more cultural obstacles at public four-year and comprehensive and community colleges than at private four-year institutions. This finding most likely relates to the more cooperative environment that often characterizes smaller institutions. In institutions with level or decreasing funding, structural obstacles seem to be more prevalent and slightly decreasing the number of partnerships. Obviously, offering incentives is more difficult within an environment of declining resources. But restructuring could serve as a lower-cost option that institutions may want to examine more often. In a campus culture of growing demands, individuals were more likely to respond that cultural barriers were even more significant obstacles. Many of the cultural obstacles relate to an ability to work together and lack of a cooperative spirit. On campuses with growing demands, faculty and staff are pressed to maintain a willingness to work toward collective goals because each individual feels greater pressure to do more. The types of students (whether mostly full-time, part-time, or half-and-half) do not appear to have an impact on obstacles. It could have been predicted that campuses with fewer full-time students might face more obstacles because it may be more challenging to integrate students into the seamless structure of the campus.

Perhaps one of the most promising findings is that having more obstacles (either cultural or structural) was not statistically related to number of successful collaborations. This is a hopeful finding. Although institutions face a host of obstacles, they are able to mitigate these challenges through the successful strategies for collaboration described earlier.

What Are the Results of Collaboration? Outcomes Assessment

Eighty percent of the institutions surveyed conduct outcomes assessment, and almost half, 45 percent, of those institutions conduct outcomes assessment of academic and student affairs collaborations. This percentage is surprising and encouraging given that it is a fairly new phenomenon for many campuses. It is hoped that the number of institutions conducting assessment will supply needed data about the positive results of these new efforts. This finding provides support and direction for future research to examine institutional assessments of their collaboration efforts. Over 33 percent of institutions also conduct focus groups and interviews providing even richer data on the impact of these new partnerships. Of those who conduct outcomes assessment, 47 institutions out of 128 examine institutional effectiveness, 28 explore student learning and development, and 25 review student achievement. Assessment is certainly prevalent on campuses, and a warehouse of data is waiting to be examined by researchers in the future.

In an open-ended question, the research team asked campuses what they perceived the benefits to be and whether their collaboration was achieving the goals and outcomes they had set forth. Although there were too few responses to report reliable trends, an improved learning environment, retention, enhanced institutional communication, culture of trust, better campus relationships, and increased attention to the work of student affairs were most often mentioned. These answers all correspond to the predicted outcomes from the literature; no new outcomes emerged (Kuh, 1996; Love and Love, 1995). In addition, those who responded felt that the collaboration was extremely beneficial given the data they had collected at this point. This result reinforces that most of the positive benefits that can emerge from these partnerships are known.

The Horse Is on the Track

Campuses are engaging in student and academic affairs collaboration to meet a host of institutional needs and note that their goals are being met. Collaborations are happening in a host of areas, from programs that are traditionally cocurricular (and would have involved some level of coordination in the past) to collaboration emerging in curricular (e.g., senior-year experience) and noncurricular (e.g., retention) areas. All types of institutions are engaging in the creation of seamless learning environments; no trend emerged for any type of institution to be more engaged in collaboration, although public four-year and comprehensive institutions tend to have had more success with a larger number of collaborations on their campuses. The process for creating collaborations between academic and student affairs divisions differs slightly based on institutional type and enrollments, but a clear set of principles arises from the study:

Begin with first-year programs and cocurricular areas that have a history of coordination. Also, be aware of institutional differences related to success with collaborations and build from areas of strength—academic advising at community colleges or community-service learning at private four-year institutions.

It is critical to first develop senior administrative support because this support appears to be related to a host of secondary strategies that are statistically related to successful collaboration.

Cultural strategies are most important. Be sure to create an environment of cooperation, develop cross-institutional dialogue, institute a common vision and goals, generate enthusiasm, examine personalities, evaluate who is being put on committees and cross-divisional work, foster involvement and a desire to increase student learning on your campus, and conduct staff development.

Do not ignore structural strategies that are significant for guiding and institutionalizing collaboration, such as a planning process, setting expectations and demanding accountability, joint or cross-divisional councils or committees, changes in job responsibilities for student affairs staff, and various forms of restructuring (e.g., developing learning communities or enrollment management).

Question the culture of student affairs that could downplay the importance of incentives and restructuring. Think of academic and student affairs collaboration within an institutional change perspective, which takes into account the size of the institution and conflicting or different institutional cultures. In other words, even if student affairs staff are motivated by the desire to work cooperatively, other members of the institution may have other motivations and perspectives that need to be taken into account.

Smaller institutions may be able to depend on leadership, but larger institutions need to rely more on restructuring, planning, incentives, and other structural strategies. Size made a difference for institutions in approaching collaboration on campus. Realize that structural strategies will be more important to fostering successful collaboration on large campuses.

Hiring new people or encouraging new leaders and change agents can reinforce cultural and structural strategies.

Do not fear institutional obstacles and barriers; merely be aware of them, especially faculty and staff time, faculty disciplinary ties, and faculty resistance. Institutional obstacles appear to play a minimal, if any, role in discouraging collaboration. Although significant obstacles exist, especially lack of time, strong faculty resistance, and lack of positive relationships among groups, the strategies being implemented can overcome these challenges.

Over time, it will be important to examine the growing data on the outcomes of collaborations between academic and student affairs data in order to illustrate the many benefits. For now, the work of continuing institutionalization remains the main task.

References

American Association for Higher Education, American College Personnel Association, and National Association of Student Personnel Administrators. *Powerful Partnerships: A Shared Responsibility for Learning*. Washington, D.C.: American Association for Higher Education, American College Personnel Association, and National Association of Student Personnel Administrators, 1998.

Johnson, C. S., and Cheatham, H. E. (eds.). *Higher Education Trends for the Next Century: Research Agenda for Student Success*. Washington, D.C.: American College Personnel Association, 1999.

Kezar, A. *Understanding and Facilitating Organizational Change in the Twenty-First Century*. ASHE-ERIC Higher Education Report, no. 28.4. San Francisco: Jossey-Bass, 2001.

Kuh, G. D. "Guiding Principles for Creating Seamless Learning Environments for Undergraduates." *Journal of College Student Development,* 1996, 37(2), 135–148. (EJ 527218)

Love, P. G., and Love, A. G. "Enhancing Student Learning: Intellectual, Social, and Emotional Integration." ASHE-ERIC Higher Education Report, no. 4. Washington, D.C.: George Washington University, Graduate School of Education and Human Development, 1995. (ED 400742)

National Association of Student Personnel Administrators. *Principles of Good Practice for Student Affairs.* Washington, D.C.: National Association of Student Personnel Administrators, 1997.

ADRIANNA KEZAR is assistant professor in the higher education administration program at the University of Maryland, College Park.

Academic and student affairs officers in New England
meet regularly to identify and develop opportunities for
collaboration.

3

Finding Points of Contact for Collaborative Work

Deborah J. Hirsch and Cathy Burack

The gap between student and academic affairs is well documented. Although originally, faculty members provided both academic and nonacademic support for students, disciplinary specialization and the growth of a higher education industry resulted in the division of these areas, with each functioning on either side of a widening chasm. Student affairs and academic affairs developed different understandings about the purposes of their work and how it should be measured. These differences and distinctions are clearly evident in the New England Resource Center for Higher Education's (NERCHE) think tanks for student and academic administrators.

NERCHE has been operating think tanks for chief student affairs officers, academic vice presidents and provosts, deans, and department chairs for over a decade. Think tank members are drawn from diverse institutions of higher education in New England—public and private, two- and four-year, rich and poor. Think tanks provide time and space for members to talk with one another about what they value and what impels them in their work and their lives. Each year NERCHE organizes a think tank around a series of topics that comprise a particular theme. Think tank members also work toward solutions for the compelling issues and problems they face in their work. Members have written articles together, presented at national conferences, and organized regional meetings on particular topics.

For NERCHE, think tank discussions provide key sources of intelligence on evolving trends, issues, and innovations. Through these discussions the center has come to understand that although the cultures and professional expectations of student affairs and academic affairs are markedly different, many of the issues they are confronting are the same.

NEW DIRECTIONS FOR HIGHER EDUCATION, no. 116, Winter 2001 © Wiley Periodicals, Inc.

53

For example, over the years, both academic and student affairs think tanks have discussed issues of assessment, technology, changing student populations, student retention, and general education. Occasionally, NERCHE has brought members of different think tanks together for rare opportunities to discuss issues of mutual interest and concern. We have observed that discussions about creating partnerships have been artificial and stilted and have tended to focus on the obstacles toward collaboration. However, when one can identify issues that cross traditional boundaries or transcend functional dichotomies, it is possible to engage groups of academic and student affairs administrators in thinking about possibilities for collaboration. These are the overlapping issues that can link student affairs and academic affairs. Assessment, technology, changing student populations, student retention, and general education are some of the common issues. We examine here these issues and the collaborative structures or forms that various partnerships have taken.

Linking Issues

Assessment. It is clear from think tank discussions that no member of the campus community, whether academic or nonacademic staff, has been immune to the external pressures for accountability and the internal pressures for improved outcomes assessment. Critics of higher education deride the rising costs, use of teaching assistants, and systems of faculty tenure and sabbaticals. The higher education community's present preoccupation with assessment and measurement of outcomes is in part a response to those who are calling for colleges to serve students both efficiently and effectively. Both student and academic affairs must be able to demonstrate program worth and quality, programmatic strengths and weaknesses, and the contribution made to institutional mission and effectiveness (Schuh and Upcraft, 2001). Providing evidence of student learning and of the value added by a college education requires collaboration and coordination across traditional campus boundaries. Student affairs in particular has been slow to quantify its work in terms of outcomes. Since the publication and adoption of *The Student Learning Imperative* (American College Personnel Association, 1994), student affairs professionals have embraced student learning as a necessary programmatic outcome. The result of this initiative has been some noteworthy efforts to document the impact of student leadership experiences in clubs and organizations on students' cognitive development (Skeat and Hirt, 2001; Schuh and Laverty, 1983). Although faculty have expertise in assessing mastery over course content and concepts, they could benefit from the skills and preparation of student affairs professionals in the areas of social and ethical development and civic responsibility. Assessment instruments that can be administered by both student and academic affairs to document the quality of the undergraduate experience can help close the gap between the two divisions. One such example is the National Survey of Student Engagement (NSSE), which was designed to assess the extent to which students are participating in educational practices that are strongly associated with high levels of learning and personal development (Bridges, Kuh, and O'Day, 2001). It can provide a meeting ground for discussion and action for academic and student affairs. Collaboration between student and academic affairs can be challenging, but it is crucial to develop shared goals for the students and a common understanding of the institution's mission.

Technology. The explosion in the forms and uses of technology has changed how subject matter is taught as well as the time and place where teaching and learning occurs. Moreover, the nature of technology on campus blurs the borders between administrative decisions and pedagogical decisions. Decision making surrounding technology has moved from issues related to academic support to those of strategic importance to the institution.

Addressing these issues in a competitive marketplace requires new cooperation and collaboration between academic and student affairs in order to focus campus discussion and decision making on technology as a way to further education and not as an end in itself. Technology should be used to serve the mission of the institution, and decisions about technology should reflect, not determine, institutional academic priorities. Technology will undoubtedly change how we think about education and how we deliver educational programs, but it is essential that academic leaders create an environment in which academic values remain in the forefront. The primary questions must focus on what an institution is seeking to achieve in teaching, research, and service. The secondary, but still highly significant, questions should address how technology can help achieve these goals and the ways in which an institution can—and will—create technology-based resources for its students, faculty, and staff. New partnerships across divisions are more critical than ever because it is no longer possible to separate academic from administrative technology; there are now important interconnections among academic technology, instructional support, and administrative system needs. Academic affairs administrators are looking to technology as a way to enliven the curriculum and pedagogy. Student affairs administrators talk about how technology can enhance campus life and community. Together, they must consider what this means in terms of academic policy, rules of student conduct, and effective use of resources.

Changing Student Population. Both academic and student affairs think tanks have discussed the impact of a changing student population on their institutions: the impact on curriculum, how courses are taught, and the kinds of academic and social support services that this new breed of students require. Today's students are more diverse in backgrounds, learning styles, and levels of preparedness. They carry their complex lives—family and work responsibilities—into the classroom. Not only is this generation of students strikingly different than its predecessors, but today's faculties and student affairs staff are also no longer the homogenous group of years past. Unlike a generation ago, faculty and student affairs staff are less apt to be white, male, and native born. They are burdened by the constraints of two-career or single-parent families and often commute some distance to work. Thus, the need for collaboration across divisions has never been more necessary: college and university faculties are themselves experiencing new stresses and pressures in addition to having to teach a new generation of students different from themselves in their motivation and abilities to access and complete their education. Student affairs professionals often serve as resources for academic and planning committees for the institutions represented in the think tanks on the needs and issues of today's students. These include providing the latest information on immigration policy, ways to rethink outreach to same-sex parents of undergraduates, legal and ethical issues in dealing with students with psychological problems, and appropriate interventions for times of crisis.

Student Retention. The decline of the traditional college-age population during the 1980s and the competitive marketplace of new for-profit providers during the 1990s brought a new era of attention to and research on the retention of college students. Whereas student retention was once an ethical issue involving equal opportunity and access to higher education, loss of talent, and student waste of time and effort, retaining students has become a practical issue linked to the survival of many higher education institutions due to a declining pool of college-age students and a plethora of new providers and distance learning. Today's students have countless options available to them and have become better informed and more sophisticated consumers regarding the costs and benefits of acquiring a degree at a particular institution. Research on college dropouts has pointed to the importance of informal interaction between students and faculty as one of the major impacts on student persistence (Tinto, 1987). Whereas student retention has often fallen to student affairs, Tinto and others show that student success is often linked to a faculty member and the classroom. The competitive marketplace and a raft of empirical studies on the causes of student attrition have created a powerful incentive for collaboration between academic and student affairs. On one campus, this collaboration takes the form of integrated teams of faculty, advisers, residence-life staff, and others who meet regularly to discuss the status of students identified as at risk for dropping out. In this way, campus professionals are often able to intervene early to get students the necessary academic support or counseling to help them be successful students.

General Education. It seems that at any given time, most colleges and universities are in the process of reviewing their general education curriculum, have just completed reviewing it, or are contemplating a curricular overhaul. And whereas faculty have traditionally held reign over course content and curricula, the general education program is a more collective endeavor, representing an overarching expression of what the college values and believes should be the hallmark of an educated person. As such, it can provide an opportunity for collaboration because no single group within the institution "owns" general education, and many of the skills and competencies identified with general education can be gained through experiences outside of the classroom (Banta and Kuh, 1998). For example, at one campus, the chief student affairs officer used the launch of a new general education program to stimulate a conversation between student and academic affairs about shared goals for students. The new academic curriculum was based on six learning objectives; student affairs staff used these objectives to examine how student activities outside of the classroom could also fulfill these learning goals. Student and academic affairs staff worked together on a companion document to the academic curriculum. The opportunity to rethink and renew the general education curriculum can provide academic and student affairs professionals with new ways of collaborating and coordinating expertise and knowledge to the benefit of student learning. By their very nature, conversations about what it means to be educated at a particular college or university need to be inclusive and expansive.

The Forms Partnerships Take

People do not usually collaborate unless they share common concerns and believe that they will be able to do their jobs more efficiently and effectively as a result. The aforementioned issues identified in both academic and student affairs think tanks provide substantive rationale for developing partnerships. These collaborations can vary from institution to institution and from partnership to partnership. However, as a whole, the collaborations between student and academic affairs tend to fall within one of three categories: structural, curricular, or programmatic. A discussion of these categories and some examples follow.

Organizational Structures. In most colleges and universities, student affairs and academic affairs occupy different organizational "silos" with separate and distinct hierarchies and reporting relationships. Even though the chief student affairs officer and the academic provost or vice president may each be a member of the president's cabinet, sharing in the overall direction and oversight of the college, they often must compete with one another for institutional resources. However, some colleges and universities are rethinking this arrangement in order to address issues of financial pressures, technology, and the new diverse student population. They are reorganizing to try to capitalize on the strengths, similarities, and complementary capacities of both student and academic affairs. Ideally, the integration of student and academic affairs would be driven by the units themselves, but the need to cut costs propels many restructuring efforts. This impetus for change inevitably creates resentments, but if the restructuring is carefully and inclusively managed, it can work. The new arrangements can team up people who, for structural reasons, have struggled against each other for resources. As a result, student and academic affairs can be linked. Institutional context and personalities aside, such structures offer new opportunities for mutual influence. For example, student affairs staff can work to help faculty become more student oriented, and faculty can help student affairs staff understand the ways in which they can contribute to student learning. On some campuses, a new professional position has been created to bridge the academic and student affairs areas. This hybrid professional, sometimes called a "learning specialist," has combined expertise in learning theory and its applications, including Web-based and distance-learning technologies (Zeller, 1999) The learning specialist is skilled in working with students in a myriad of learning environments within and beyond classroom walls.

Other restructuring efforts connect various units within the academic and student affairs arenas that are complementary in focus and purpose. For example, the counseling center may be linked to the psychology or counseling departments. A center or program for international studies may be linked to international studies or foreign language departments. Yet another structural possibility for joining student and academic affairs can be achieved through the creative use of space. A student center, for example, can be built as a place where students' academic and social needs are met so that learning is seen to occur both within and outside of the classroom. By housing offices for both faculty and student affairs staff under one roof, the chances abound for informal interaction that can seed future collaboration. One reason for this is that partnerships are often formed among individuals who have a relationship with one another. Shared space can foster the development of friendships and mutual respect among both academic and nonacademic colleagues.

Whatever the configuration, the leadership of an institution plays a critical role in both encouraging and rewarding collaborative efforts that are characterized by good communication and power sharing. Among think tank institutions these most often take the forms of joint cabinet positions, joint membership on key institutional committees, and shared roles in institutional strategic planning.

Curricular Innovations. A number of recent curricular offerings have created unique roles for faculty and student affairs staff to work together in ways that enhance student learning. Service learning offers one such opportunity for collaboration. Students who wish to work in community-based settings need assistance in finding suitable placements, as well as close supervision and opportunities for thoughtful reflection and connection to their academic learning. The time and effort required to find placements, monitor student learning, and integrate that learning into the classroom are often more than a faculty member is able or prepared to give. In addition, goals of service-learning programs include the development of citizenship, social responsibility, and moral development—modes more closely identified with student affairs work. It is a natural extension for student affairs professionals who have had long experience with out-of-class learning through student internships, career planning, and community service to work in partnership with faculty to connect students' service with their courses and academic learning. On one campus a cocurricular transcript was developed for each student to capture the educational experiences that occur outside of the curriculum. Thus, a student gets "credit" for service-learning experiences that do not take place within the context of a course as well as for involvement and leadership in student organizations. Bridging the classroom with the out-of-class experiences redefines the parameters with which faculty and student affairs professionals work with one another. They become partners in the effort to support student learning.

Learning communities feature intentional groupings of students, coordinated scheduling, collaborative or cooperative learning techniques, and courses linked conceptually around common themes. Sometimes learning communities incorporate a living-learning or residential college component in which cohorts of students take a common set of courses and live in a residence or on a floor of a residence hall. Learning that begins in a classroom and extends to the dining hall, dorm room, and social activities creates a seamless intellectual experience for students. Several of the think tank members' campuses have used a variation of the learning community to create linked courses in which cohorts of students take classes that are developed along a certain theme. One campus designated a floor in one of the residence halls in which residential-life staff developed programs that complemented the material that students were learning in their courses. Faculty who taught in the program were invited to dine informally with the students on a regular basis. These campuses found that learning communities were an effective method for fostering collaborative learning environments in which both faculty and student affairs staff can contribute to and support the creation of vital and intellectual communities for students both in and out of the classroom. Not only do faculty and student affairs staff who become part of the learning community redefine and expand many of the traditional notions of their professional roles and responsibilities, but research indicates that students who participate in a learning community do better academically and are more likely to graduate (Pike, Schroeder, and Berry, 1997).

Programmatic Activities. A number of programmatic activities that support and enhance the academic, in-classroom learning experience have worked their way into many, if not most, campuses. These include orientation and first-year programs, leadership activities, and student programs that require intensive staff and faculty participation.

Freshman orientation and first-year programs are arenas in which academic and student affairs can collaborate to orient and support students entering an academic community. The trend on most campuses is to offer an orientation, often followed by a semester or yearlong course focused on a common academic experience along with practical skills and advice about becoming a successful student. Reflection is a critical component of these courses. One campus has found that these opportunities for reflection on the students' educational experiences—and most students report that their most powerful educational experiences take place outside of the classroom—help faculty connect curricular components with other educational goals. These courses provide opportunities for faculty members and student affairs staff to work together to plan, coordinate, and coteach small groups of students. In these settings faculty and student affairs staff often develop a greater understanding of and respect for the expertise each other brings to the institution. For student affairs staff this is especially important because they often feel that the institution devalues their work. These collaborations have a powerful impact on students in the form of increased student retention, improved academic performance, and stronger institutional affiliation.

Leadership programs provide another natural vehicle for collaboration. Skill-development workshops are often offered to student leaders to develop their capacity to run meetings, budget, and manage finances, in addition to public speaking and team building. When faculty are enlisted to participate in these programs, students can gain a richer understanding of leadership theory and styles, as well as the organizational psychology of groups (Fried, 1999). These same leadership programs in turn often provide the campus with a pool of students who can ably serve on college and university committees.

Student activities, clubs, and organizations are traditionally areas in which faculty involvement and participation have been sporadic and haphazard at best. These groups have had to rely on those faculty with a special interest in the organization or in relating to students in out-of-class activities. As noted previously, this practice continues despite the research on student retention and persistence that supports the involvement of faculty with students in out-of-class experiences. Still, there is great potential for faculty and student affairs to interact and collaborate so that students' out-of-class time not only supports classroom learning but also extends and expands it. Traditionally, there have been real obstacles beyond time and interest to faculty participation. A reward system that fails to recognize their participation provides a strong disincentive for faculty to become involved in student activities. In fact, this system may penalize them for their involvement. Thus it is crucial that as collaborative activities are developed, they must be meaningful, relevant, and rewarding for both the faculty member and the students.

Conclusion

NERCHE's academic and student affairs think tanks have raised many of the important issues with which institutions of higher education are grappling. As they respond to the many pressures that are being applied from both outside and inside the academy, the academic and student affairs professionals who formerly occupied either of these distinct areas are now spending more time in the corridors between these two divisions—sharing interests and responsibilities in ways they never have before. Coexistence can no longer be the goal; instead, academic and student affairs must find new ways of relating and working together in order to meet the specific challenges presented by new and different students, new technologies, and new providers—all of which have changed where and how postsecondary education is delivered. Remaining competitive, and indeed surviving in this changed landscape, requires openness, flexibility, and innovative strategies and structures for working across divisions toward the goal of an enhanced learning environment for students. Each professional brings to the table specialized knowledge and skills. What they share is a common goal of student learning. With that in mind, they need to develop an appreciation for the complementary roles they play in the education process. When they do this, they discover firsthand what the college impact research shows—that cognitive and affective development are inextricably intertwined (Banta and Kuh, 1998).

References

American College Personnel Association. *The Student Learning Imperative: Implications for Student Affairs*. Washington, D.C.: American College Personnel Association, 1994.

Banta, T. W., and Kuh, G. D. "A Missing Link in Assessment: Collaboration Between Academic and Student Affairs Professionals." *Change,* 1998, *30*(2), 40–46.

Bridges, B., Kuh, G., and O'Day, P. "The National Survey of Student Engagement." *NASPA's NetResults*. Washington, D.C.: National Assocation of Student Personnel Association, 2001.

Fried, J. "Two Steps to Creative Campus Collaboration." *AAHE Bulletin,* 1999, *51*(7), 10–12.

Pike, G. R., Schroeder, C. C., and Berry T. R. "Enhancing the Educational Impact of Residence Halls: The Relationship Between Residential Learning Communities and First Year College Experiences and Persistence." *Journal of College Student Development,* 1997, *38,* 609–621.

Schuh, J. H., and Laverty, M. "The Perceived Long-Term Benefits of Holding a Significant Student Leadership Position." *Journal of College Student Personnel,* 1983, *24*(1), 28–32.

Schuh, J. H., and Upcraft, M. L. "Assessment Practice in Student Affairs: An Application Manual." *The Jossey-Bass Higher and Adult Education Series*. San Francisco: Jossey Bass, 2001. (ED 447389)

Skeat, C., and Hirt, J. B. "Cognitive Development and Student Leadership Experiences." *NASPA's NetResults*. [http://www.naspa.org/NETResults]. 2001.

Tinto, V. *Leaving College: Rethinking the Causes and Cures of Student Attrition.* Chicago: University of Chicago Press, 1987.
Zeller, William J. "The Learning Specialist." *About Campus,* 1999, *4*(4), 31–32.

DEBORAH J. HIRSCH *is director of the New England Resource Center for Higher Education, University of Massachusetts Boston.*

CATHY BURACK *is associate director of the New England Resource Center for Higher Education, University of Massachusetts Boston.*

4

The factors affecting the creation of academic and student affairs collaborations display empirical profiles.

Organizational Models and Facilitators of Change: Providing a Framework for Student and Academic Affairs Collaboration

Adrianna Kezar

I spent the first five years of my higher education career working for the vice president for student affairs at a large research university. During this time, I also had an assortment of assignments in academic affairs; I worked for the Center for the Research on Learning and Teaching, for the Academic Senate, and for the Center for Women. I had the opportunity to be an insider on both the student affairs and academic affairs parts of campus, areas that have been traditionally divided. One project that I coordinated was the Welcome Program for incoming first-year students. This campus-wide activity required coordination between academic affairs and student affairs. As I planned this event each year, I wondered why it was so difficult to accomplish. When I worked on programs that were within either academic affairs or student affairs, there were far fewer problems. I pondered what could ease collaboration. I searched for books or articles on the topic but could not find any that had evidence to support their assertions for using a particular approach to collaboration. This conundrum led me to conduct a study of academic and student affairs collaboration and to examine models might help facilitate a closer working relationship.

In this chapter, I review three prominent process change models—Kuh's seamless change, planned change, and restructuring—that have been advocated for creating a seamless learning environment. I also describe whether the empirical research I conducted support that these models aid in establishing collaboration. By comparing and contrasting the ability of institutions

NEW DIRECTIONS FOR HIGHER EDUCATION, no. 116, Winter 2001 © Wiley Periodicals, Inc.

to successfully use several change frameworks, we can develop a better understanding of how to create a seamless environment. The results described in this chapter are from the same study conducted by the Educational Resources Information Center (ERIC), National Association of Student Personnel Administrators (NASPA), and American College Personnel Association (ACPA) reviewed in Chapter Two. I also examine possible difference in using these models by institutional characteristics such as size, mission, enrollments, and funding. (The design of the study is discussed in Chapter Two of this volume.) The present chapter ends with a description of a model for successfully creating academic and student affairs partnerships.

Theories of Change

This section provides an overview of why the three models of change were chosen to frame the study. In order to place these models in context, it is important to describe briefly the theories that have been used to conceptualize them. Cultural theories suggest that the alteration of values and meaning systems are the most important for creating change. Change tends to be long term, complex, nonlinear, irrational, not predictable, ongoing, and dynamic (Smircich, 1983). Human relations theories suggest that change is best facilitated through people and consider development and training to be the core strategies; Kuh's model draws heavily on both cultural and human relation theories. Theorists working within the tradition of rational theories of change conceptualize leadership, planning, and other scientific management tools as the key to creating change; the planned change model evolved out of rational theories of change. The restructuring or reengineering model evolved out of the structural theories of change, which focus on how institutional policy and practice shape employee behavior and how embedded patterns of behavior prevent change from occurring. Researchers suggest that altering institutional structures is the most successful approach to institutionalizing change.

I used Kuh's model, planned change, and restructuring as a foundation and framework for this study for a number of reasons. First, they provide a way to investigate the main theories described in the literature on change over the last thirty years: cultural, structural, and rational theories. Second, they incorporate three core target areas for change: values or beliefs, processes, and structures. Third, by using these models, the study could examine the explanatory power of structural and cultural theories of change, the two most often cited approaches. Finally, by focusing on these three models, the study could address whether a blended approach to change, by combining models with varying focuses on values, leadership, and structures, might best facilitate collaboration.

Kuh's Model for Developing a Seamless Environment

Few studies have examined strategies for enhancing collaboration in higher education institutions; George Kuh's work is a notable exception. Kuh developed the principles that form the basis of his model mostly from the literature and from experience; he notes that his principles are "influenced heavily by [his] experience working with several dozen colleges and universities over the past decade" (1996, p. 137). Kuh developed six principles to guide institutions in integrating the curriculum and extracurriculum: (1) generate enthusiasm for institutional renewal, (2) create a common vision of learning, (3) develop a common language, (4) foster collaboration and cross-functional dialogue, (5) examine the influence of student cultures on student learning, and (6) focus on systematic change.

The common element in each of the six principles is altering values through campus-wide dialogue. This dialogue is crucial to creating a common vision with which to provide a seamless learning environment for students. Generating enthusiasm refers to developing champions or change agents for the initiatives that help provide buy-in for others; capitalizing on new campus leaders is seen as advantageous for the development of enthusiasm because they come with fresh energy. By creating a common vision of learning, an institution strives to have people think about learning in the same way; there are diverse perspectives about the nature of learning and the best way to promote it. Developing a common language is important because it requires people to examine the mental models that shape their practice. By reviewing our language and embedded values, we are also altering behavior. Fostering collaboration and cross-functional dialogue is imperative for organizational learning. Organizational learning occurs by developing a common language and engaging in ongoing conversation about the work of the institution. Finally, focus on systemic change is an effort to view the institution as a whole because change is difficult without an understanding of all the structures, factors, and cultures. Most of these principles reflect assumptions from the cultural and human relations theories of change. The study described in this chapter did not examine the influence of student cultures on student learning because this principle did not relate directly to the notion of change strategies.

Kuh's set of principles for change mostly reflects human relations theories such as working in teams, learning, and vision setting. In addition, there are elements of cultural theories of change in his emphasis on vision, language, and generating enthusiasm. Kuh also describes his model as compatible with environmental change theories, in which change is random, haphazard, and in response to the environment or context; it is often unplanned. This contrasts with planned change, in which a seamless environment is not created by chance encounters by people on campus but by intentional response to management or leadership. The outcome of the change process within Kuh's model is a new set of values or norms that guide people's behavior.

From the description of Kuh's model, one might predict that smaller institutions and institutions with more homogenous cultures could more easily use his model for creating academic and student affairs partnerships because establishing a common vision or language is easier in these cases. Values are complex to change and to make "common" within heterogeneous environments.

Planned Change

Planned change focuses on the way that leaders play an instrumental role in creating change (Brill and Worth, 1997; Carnall, 1995). The key strategies described within planned change models are leadership or senior administrative support, planning, strategy, clear goals and objectives, setting expectations and demanding accountability, use of outside expertise such as consultants, incentives, staff development, and marketing and promotion of change (Brill and Worth, 1997; Carnall, 1995; Huber and Glick, 1993). This model focuses on altering processes (e.g., assessment, planning, budgeting) and intentionality, in contrast to Kuh's model, which focuses on altering values. Furthermore, Kuh's model assumes that change is a result of random events and conversations, whereas the planned change model suggests that random haphazard change does not lead to substantive organizational change. Instead, leaders and change agents play a central role in ensuring that change is functional and benefits the organization by assessing the environment or analyzing stakeholder's needs. Furthermore, researchers within this model suggest that change initiated by random events or environmental influences is often dysfunctional (Brill and Worth, 1997; Carnall, 1995; Huber and Glick, 1993).

Planned change differs from cultural or human relations theories by emphasizing the importance of goals and a planning process as opposed to conversation and dialogue. Conversations should be guided, implementation needs to be outlined clearly with expectations, processes need mandated accountability mechanisms, and training alters people's attitudes—allowing them to move in new directions and to follow the planning process (Carr, Hard, and Trahant, 1996). Although the emphasis on staff development is shared with human relations models of change, the outcome of the change process is a set of accomplished goals and new processes. This outcome contrasts with Kuh's model, which considers changed values as the end goal (or organizational structures, as will be described in the next section). Structural changes often occur as part of planned change models, but the restructuring itself is not seen as the key element to creating change. Also within this model, change is essentially never seen as complete because there are always ways to improve processes.

One may predict that planned change models are most important for community colleges and comprehensive institutions with medium to large enrollments, with a larger percentage of part-time students, and with an institutional culture of growing demands (e.g., where faculty and staff are being asked to take on additional responsibilities without promotion or compensation). Within these larger, often ambiguous environments, planning, goal setting, assessment, and senior administrative support all seem critical to providing needed guideposts in the change process. These environments involve complex processes that can be difficult to understand, let alone change. In addition, maintaining motivation for change is difficult without directives and incentives from leaders. In a culture of growing demands, it is important for senior administrative staff to set direction; employees may seek guidance in setting priorities because there is more work than they can possibly accomplish. Academic and student affairs collaboration seems unlikely within this environment without support, direction, and incentives.

Restructuring

Within restructuring or reengineering models, organizations are seen as predominantly made up of an organizational chart that establishes division of labor, roles, rules, regulations, relationships among people, and objectives (Brill and Worth, 1997; Carnall, 1995; Huber and Glick, 1993). Problems within organizations are essentially defined as structural dilemmas needing attention. For example, if communication is poor, lines of communication need to be altered, which means having people report to different individuals within the organizational chart. A problem of collaboration can be addressed either through better structures for coordination or by breaking down the division of labor and decreasing specialization (Brill and Worth, 1997). Because these organizing principles are embedded into roles and functions, the best way to alter these underlying assumptions is through structural modification. Not surprisingly, the outcome of the change process is new structures or organizing principles.

Reengineering or restructuring focuses on modifying aspects of the organizational structure as the key to creating change (Guskin, 1996). The leader's role is to inventory and assess the organizational structures and to think about ways to structure differently. Mapping processes is a key management technique for helping to reengineer, which entails cross-functional teams meeting for extended periods of time to describe and chart a process from beginning to end, with all divisions involved, hearing the processes of other functional areas and identifying ways that structures can be altered collectively. Technological advancements, new products, retrained employees, cost cutting, and other changes are facilitated by leaders who create a technology office, provide a new human resources office, or reduce the number of offices in charge of a particular function. The key in reengineering models is the alteration of organizational structure, which will alter employee behavior.

Some researchers suggest that restructuring may be even more important among larger organizations in which the complexity and size make structures critical for creating order. Bureaucracies themselves developed because of the perceived need to create more stable and effective functioning within the increasingly large organizations of the industrial age (Morgan, 1986). Researchers in this tradition believe that change among individuals cannot simply be facilitated through leadership or communication because the institutional structures themselves are embedded with roles, rules, and barriers that will prevent the changes that leaders or groups try to accomplish. They acknowledge that leaders or change agents are important but note

Table 4.1. Summary of Three Organizational Models of Change

Category	Kuh	Planned Change	Restructuring
Theory Base	Cultural and human relations	Rational	Structural
Main Strategies	Altering values, traditions, language, and vision	Goals, planning process, and assessment	Altering roles and functions: inventory and assess structures
Target of activities	Collective effort related to values and beliefs	Leadership	Organizational chart, operating procedures
Outcome	New set of values or norms	Accomplished goals and new processes	New structures or organizing principles

that leaders are transient, whereas structures are more permanent and more likely to sustain institutionalization of change. They observe that new leaders come in with ideas but that those ideas often die as soon as the leaders leave because their charismatic presence is no longer there to sustain the change (Morgan, 1986). In addition, the new set of values that the leaders may have established tends to disappear and the traditional structures soon reinforce previous approaches.

It is hypothesized that comprehensive institutions, universities, campuses with an institutional culture in which research is a priority, and campuses with large enrollments will be more likely to use and be successful with structural strategies of change. Institutions that offer graduate degrees and have a strong research orientation are often splintered into subgroups and conflicting camps. Kuh's strategies are unlikely to bring needed common vision or enthusiasm among individuals with such differing perspectives. Furthermore, these different cultures are embedded in institutional cultures that separate labor more distinctly than on smaller campuses where people are more likely to work together. The larger size and complexity often associated with these institutions suggest that strategies need to address fundamental institutional structures to create change.

Table 4.1 summarizes some of the major aspects of the three models tested within this study.

Study Results

The ERIC Clearinghouse on Higher Education, NASPA, and ACPA jointly conducted a national survey study of academic and student affairs collaborations. The survey examined a broad range of issues related to collaboration. This chapter focuses on a few sections of the survey related to what made these collaborations successful, new structures or models used to facilitate collaboration, strategies that were most successful, and institutional characteristics. Chief student affairs officers were used as the sample for the survey; 128 individuals returned the survey, for a survey response of 49 percent.

Usage and Success. Strategies within the planned change model were most commonly used, with over 661 responses—216 (33 percent) being very successful, 275 (42 percent) as successful, and 170 (25 percent) being occasionally successful. Strategies within the Kuh model were the next most used approaches, with 182 responses (35 percent of those who used these strategies) reporting being very successful, 260 (51 percent) being successful, and only 73 (14 percent) noting that these strategies were only occasionally successful. Restructuring strategies were the least often used, with 44 responses (14 percent of those who used these strategies) stating these strategies were very successful, 110 (38 percent) as successful, and 146 (49 percent) as occasionally successful. Planned change appears to be so strongly represented because leadership is the most often used strategy for creating this type of change. Leadership was followed by campus-wide dialogue, making Kuh's model high in use. It is important to note, however, that use of a particular model does not mean that change was successful.

Kuh's model was perceived as slightly more successful than planned change strategies, yet this difference is marginal (2 percent higher on very successful and 9 percent higher on moderately successful). Restructuring was seen as the least successful; over half the individuals who used these strategies responded that they were only occasionally successful.

Examination of the individual change strategies, for example, staff development, for differential impact on facilitating collaboration revealed patterns of perceived importance. In terms of usage, senior administrative support and leadership was by far the most often cited strategy for success, with 80 percent reporting that it was a very successful strategy for creating partnerships between academic and student affairs. There was a statistically significant variance by institutional type, with universities/comprehensive institutions citing senior administrative support as less important than the two other institutional types (community colleges and liberal arts colleges). Senior administrative support appeared to play the most significant role in private four-year, followed by community, colleges.

Of the other individual strategies, a combination of planned change and Kuh strategies were found to be critical for developing change: cross-institutional dialogue (Kuh; 57 percent very successful, 36 percent moderately successful), setting expectations (planned change; 44 percent very successful, 53 percent moderately successful), generating enthusiasm (Kuh; 41 percent very successful, 56 percent moderately successful), creating a common vision (planned change; 39 percent very successful, 54 percent moderately successful), staff development (planned change; 40 percent very successful, 99 percent moderately successful), and planning (planned change; 30 percent very successful, 60 percent moderately successful). These findings suggest that the human and relational principles outlined in Kuh's model should be paired with some concrete management practices offered within

the planned change model. The three most highly rated restructuring strategies were restructuring (66 percent very or moderately successful), combining fiscal resources (63 percent very or moderately successful), and incentives
(53 percent very or moderately successful), but these strategies were significantly lower than the planned change and Kuh strategies in both usage and
perceived success. Clearly, altering structures to create more collaboration
was not seen as enough to alter the environment to embrace collaboration.

The next analysis examined the relationship of the Kuh's, planned
change, and restructuring models to the actual number of successful collaborations in order to determine the efficacy of these models for facilitating collaboration on campus and to move beyond self-perception. In
significance tests of number of successful collaborations with the three
change models, Kuh and planned change have a significant relationship
with the number of successful partnerships. The more campuses used Kuh
or planned change strategies, the greater were the number of successful and
very successful collaborations. Restructuring was not significantly related
to increased numbers of collaborative partnerships. However, there was a
pattern for curricular collaborations; those who used more restructuring
strategies were more likely to have six or more successful collaborations.
This is not surprising since successful curricular collaborations may involve
an examination of tenure policies or reward structures to support long
established patterns within the institution.

There is a relationship between use of Kuh strategies and number of
very successful collaborations; campuses that tended have greater numbers
of very successful collaborations tended to use more Kuh strategies. This
trend is revealed in the following data: 92 percent of campuses that had six
or more very successful (and successful) collaborations used more than three
Kuh strategies, 75 percent of those that had three to five very successful (and
successful) collaborations had used three or more Kuh strategies, and 68 percent with one or more very successful (and successful) collaborations had
used three or more Kuh strategies. This contrasts with only 8 percent of
respondents who had six or more successful collaborations that used only
one or two of the Kuh strategies. The percentages were virtually the same
across both curricular and cocurricular collaborative activities. The previous
percentages were for cocurricular. The following are the percentages for curricular collaborative activities: 92 percent for six or more, 75 percent for
three to five, and 65 percent for one or two successful collaborations.

A relationship also exists between planned change strategies and the
number of successful collaborations: 80 percent that had six or more very
successful (and successful) collaborations successfully used more than five
or more planned strategies, 56 percent of those that had three to five very
successful (and successful) collaborations had used five or more planned
change strategies, and 53 percent that had one or more successful (and
successful) collaborations had used five or more planned change strategies. This contrasts with only 20 percent of individual who had six or
more successful collaborations that had used four or less of the planned

change strategies. The percentages are relatively close across curricular and cocurricular types of collaborative activities. For curricular collaborations 79 percent had six or more, 64 percent had three to five, and 38 percent had one or two successful collaborations. There appears to be an even stronger relationship between using planned change models with curricular collaborations. Again, curricular collaborations may need to be supported by institutional leadership and expectations for employees to be successful.

Institutional Differences. There were few institutional variations. Private four-year institutions were the least likely to be able to use Kuh strategies successfully; 64 percent had success using three to five strategies and 35 percent had success using less than three. This is in contrast to community colleges and universities/comprehensive institutions where both reported that 84 percent were successful using three or more strategies. Universities/comprehensive institutions had more success with planned change: 70 percent used five or more planned change strategies. Private four-year institutions (54 percent) and community colleges (58 percent) were less likely to use planned change models. Restructuring was not related to institutional type; all rated that they used this strategy with limited success.

Enrollments, funding, and institutional culture were not significantly related to use of Kuh's, planned change, or restructuring models of change. Across enrollment levels, all institutions tended to use the same number of Kuh strategies; approximately 75 percent used four or more and 25 percent used three or less. Planned change appeared to be used more often by larger institutions (ten thousand and above), with 74 percent using five or more strategies, as opposed to 52 percent at institutions with enrollments between one thousand and ten thousand. There is a similar pattern among restructuring strategies with 47 percent of institutions of ten thousand or more using two or more restructuring strategies, 28 percent at enrollment levels of three thousand to ten thousand using two or more restructuring strategies successfully, and 23 percent at one thousand to three thousand using two or more restructuring strategies. Kuh strategies were more likely to be used successfully on campuses that prioritized learning: 93 percent used three or more strategies successfully compared to 75 percent for institutions that prioritized research and 73 percent for those in which growing demands took precedence. Planned change was used and perceived to be equally successful across institutional cultures; this may relate to the general importance of processes, such as planning or setting expectations, that are critical across institutional cultures.

Identifying a Model for Student and Academic Affairs Collaboration

The data indicate that Kuh's model is most closely aligned with success for both curricular and cocurricular collaborations. However, Kuh's model was seen as almost equally successful to planned change models. Of the twenty individual strategies, three of Kuh's strategies were found critical for developing change: cross-institutional dialogue (ranked second), generating enthusiasm (fourth) and creating a common vision (fifth). Three elements that made planned change extremely important for creating partnerships: leadership (first), setting expectations/holding people accountable (third), and staff development (sixth). It appears that institutions that combine elements of both models may experience the most success.

In open-ended responses, most people mentioned that new people and leaders had come to campus, which helped significantly in making the change. Bringing in new leaders or change agents was not a choice on the survey, so the importance of leadership may have been underestimated. Even without this choice, however, senior administrative support/leadership was seen as the number-one strategy for creating change. Thus planned change may be even more important to creating change than demonstrated in this study.

Although the study found that restructuring was not related to successful number of collaborations, it may be that fewer institutions are using restructuring strategies, which in turn may have affected the ability to adequately identify their impact. There were also many smaller colleges represented in the sample, which could have impacted the usage and importance of restructuring strategies. Some evidence in the data suggests that restructuring was more successful and used more on larger campuses. Moreover, open-ended survey responses about strategies not noted on the survey, but that were successful for facilitating collaboration, identified the following restructuring areas: enrollment management, dual admissions processes, incorporation of business process reengineering, joint councils, and learning communities (learning communities appeared on the survey as a type of collaboration, but not specifically as a strategy). These strategies were not specific choices on the survey and may represent a host of structural approaches that are being successfully used on campuses. Future studies that focus on the use of restructuring strategies may uncover some valuable approaches that can help guide campus efforts. However, in this study, structural strategies in general were not related to the success on these campuses.

This study attempted to move beyond self-perception of successful strategies by examining relationships between strategies and the number of successful collaborations. Because restructuring tends to be used less and is perhaps underestimated in effectiveness, this analysis may help shed light on the efficacy of restructuring theories or point more definitively to the strength of the Kuh's and planned change models. The statistically significant relationship of Kuh and planned change with the number of successful partnerships illustrates the power of these models. In contrast, restructuring was not statistically significant with the number of successful collaborations, reinforcing is seeming lesser importance. Planned change appeared to be even more significant among curricular types of collaboration. Perhaps there is a need for senior administrative support (accompanied by institutional focus and resources) in order to develop expectations for a change that will alter current operations more drastically.

Institutional Variations

There was only one statistically significant variation by institutional type: the importance of leadership. Community colleges and private four-year institutions identified leadership as an even more successful strategy for the development of partnerships. This finding supports structural theory, which notes that the size of institutions diffuses the efficacy of leadership. Other predicted variations such as greater use of restructuring approaches at larger institutions or more usage of Kuh's model at smaller institutions did not emerge in the data as statistically significant.

Some of these predicted variations were apparent in the data, however, and may be identifiable in a study with a larger sample size. For instance, there was a pattern for universities/comprehensive institutions and institutions with enrollment of ten thousand or more to have more success with planning. This finding aligns with the literature on planned change that suggests that larger, more complex organizations will need careful planning, goals, accountability standards, staff development, and incentives in order to create change. There is a similar pattern in restructuring: institutions of ten thousand or more using two or more restructuring strategies successfully.

Some of the trends in the data were contrary to the predicted patterns. For example, private four-year institutions were the least likely to be able to successfully use Kuh strategies. Perhaps they did not need to use these strategies because they have more of a common language and vision. The success of community colleges with Kuh strategies was also surprising; the prediction was that in an environment with few full-time faculty and students, it might be more difficult to create a common vision and language and to initiate cross-campus dialogue.

Conclusion

This study left me with a better understanding of how to more successfully facilitate collaboration in the future. In the next project or program in which I work with both academic and student affairs, I will attempt a blended approach or model that combines strategies from Kuh's (generating enthusiasm, developing a common vision) and planned change (promoting change, staff development) models. I also know which specific strategies within these various change models have been most effective at creating change, such as cross-institutional dialogue and setting expectations. I may need to challenge or educate a colleague who focuses exclusively on restructuring as the way to create collaboration. I will also be attuned to some institutional differences. Because I am at a larger institution with an enrollment of over ten thousand, I may need to rely less on leadership and focus instead on planning and restructuring. If I move to a smaller institution, leadership and the planned change model will be more important for me to consider. Although there is certainly much more to learn about creating successful partnerships, I now have some proven strategies that have worked nationally on which to draw.

References

Brill, P. L., and Worth, R. *The Four Levers of Corporate Change.* New York: American Management Association, 1997.

Carnall, C. A. *Managing Change in Organizations.* (2nd ed.) London: Prentice Hall, 1995.

Carr, D., Hard, K., and Trahant, W. *Managing the Change Process: A Field Book for Change Agents, Consultants, Team Leaders, and Reengineering Managers.* New York: McGraw-Hill, 1996.

Guskin, A. E. "Facing the Future: The Change Process in Restructuring Universities." *Change,* 1996, 28(4), 27–37.

Huber, G. P., and Glick, W. H. *Organizational Change and Redesign: Ideas and Insights for Improving Performance.* New York: Oxford University Press, 1993.

Kuh, G. D. "Guiding Principles for Creating Seamless Learning Environments for Undergraduates." *Journal of College Student Development,* 1996, 37(2), 135–148. (EJ 527218)

Morgan, G. *Images of Organization.* Newbury Park, Calif.: Sage, 1986.

Smircich, L. "Organizations as Shared Meanings." In L. R. Pondy, P. J. Frost, G. Morgan, and T. C. Dandridge (eds.), *Organizational Symbolism.* Greenwich, Conn.: JAI, 1983.

ADRIANNA KEZAR is assistant professor in the higher education administration program at the University of Maryland, College Park.

5

Thoughtful collaborations between student and academic affairs enhance the student learning environment.

Facilitative Strategies in Action

Thara M. A. Fuller and Adrian K. Haugabrook

Higher education as an enterprise has been in constant transition. Universities and colleges face ever-increasing competition from a new generation of education providers as well as scrutiny by stakeholders. More recently, institutions have had to focus on issues of effectiveness, responsibility, accountability, outcome measures, and program assessment and evaluation. These and other issues have arisen in a new climate: resources for institutions of higher learning are becoming not more bountiful but more restrictive, particularly in the public arena. This is occurring at a time when the common perception of higher education is low, intrusion and intervention by boards of trustees, governing bodies, and legislatures is high, and all are calling for institutions to be more effective and efficient in achieving specific performance outcomes. One major performance outcome includes enhancing institutional climate so that it is more conducive to increasing the quality of student learning. Ender, Newton, and Caple (1996) assert that institutional leadership must recognize that student affairs can be integral to promoting student learning and academic success.

Student affairs professionals have responded by attempting to position the profession as partners in the learning process for students. The focus of the work of student affairs professionals has been to be more deliberate in facilitating and affecting learning outcomes for students. This emphasis is evident in documents such as *The Student Learning Imperative: Implications for Student Affairs* (American College Personnel Association, 1994) and *Powerful Partnerships: A Shared Responsibility for Learning* (American Association for Higher Education, American College Personnel Association, and National Association of Student Personnel Administrators, 1998). These documents call for greater collaboration between academic affairs and student affairs and

NEW DIRECTIONS FOR HIGHER EDUCATION, no. 116, Winter 2001 © Wiley Periodicals, Inc.

for more purposeful incorporation of learning outcomes in student affairs programming.

This chapter rests on the assertion that student affairs programming directly affects student learning and that thoughtful collaborations between student affairs and academic affairs further enhance the student learning environment and advance an institution toward shared responsibility for student development and achievement. The purpose of the chapter is to provide brief case studies of programs at the University of Massachusetts Boston (UMass Boston) that link student affairs and academic affairs and to present these cases as examples of multiple strategies that could be applied at other institutions developing such collaborations. The discussion of these case studies highlights four areas:

1. The framework of learning outcomes underlying the collaborations
2. The ways in which the expertise of student affairs professionals contribute to the attainment of the objectives
3. Approaches for developing productive partnerships across departments and divisions
4. Approaches for gaining institutional support for collaborative programs

Both long-term strategic planning and spontaneous discovery contributed to the development of the three programs discussed here. One of the most important lessons learned from these experiences is to be alert for opportunities and potential partners that were not in the original plan. Successful collaboration is an ongoing process and requires constant attention to the interpersonal dynamics among the team players. Those who take a leadership role in forming collaborations need to give high priority to maintaining solid working relationships even as they focus on the content of the programs.

At UMass Boston a full-scale review of the programs in the Division of Student Affairs in 1998 and 1999 laid the foundation for significant restructuring and new program development in close cooperation with the Division of Academic Affairs and other units. The university's executive leadership actively supported, as an integral part of the restructuring, collaboration between the Divisions of Student Affairs and Academic Affairs. The Office of the Dean of Students took the initiative in designing programmatic and structural elements that would maximize the expertise and resources of both divisions. The following three initiatives exemplify this redesign:

1. The Beacon Leadership Project is a credit- and competency-bearing, intensive program of instructional seminars and experiential learning, built on an existing cocurricular program.
2. The Diversity Research Initiative, initially temporary and grant funded, was re-envisioned as a fully institutionalized program to develop undergraduate research that informs UMass Boston's efforts to meet its mission and respond to the needs of the diverse student body.

3. The Beacon Think Tank, a brand-new program, was created to provide a forum for student and faculty discussions on issues related to their experiences as citizens of the university and society.

As the following discussion explains, the development of each of these initiatives occurred through close cooperation among key individuals. Advisory committees with representation from throughout the university played critical roles in establishing the legitimacy of the endeavors, building broad cross-divisional support and ensuring the feasibility and quality of the programs. In each case, the programmatic innovations led to, or developed in concert with, certain structural changes that enhanced the effectiveness of the collaboration between the Divisions of Student Affairs and Academic Affairs.

The Urban Mission Drives Restructuring

UMass Boston is a commuter campus with a total enrollment of over thirteen thousand students, of whom 30 percent are members of a minority group. Over half the students are enrolled part-time; many are juggling jobs and raising families. Fifty-nine percent are first-generation college students, and the median age for undergraduates is twenty-four. The reorganization of the Division of Student Affairs at UMass Boston, critical in setting the stage for cross-divisional collaboration, was triggered in part by staff turnover in the division and in part by the emerging priority that each division clearly demonstrate how it advances the university's urban mission and a shared ethos for continuous student learning. In speeches and committee meetings, the executive leadership frequently invoked this mission as a guiding principle for the university to serve the needs of an increasingly diverse commuter population and to educate students to be responsible citizens of the larger community.

The restructuring of the Division of Student Affairs and the development of the programs outlined in this chapter took place in the context of these larger campus discussions about the university's mission. During the review of the programming in student affairs, it became clear that a direct and effective way to create a "shared ethos" for student learning would be purposeful partnerships with the Division of Academic Affairs. The assistant dean of students then laid out a plan to establish such partnerships. There were three main approaches: (1) revitalizing existing programs in student affairs by renewing the emphasis on learning outcomes and encouraging faculty to contribute their expertise, (2) identifying programs in academic affairs that might be enhanced by the contributions of student affairs professionals, and (3) developing a cross-divisional team to design new programs whose outcomes incorporate both student development and student learning.

The Beacon Leadership Project: The Re-Visioning of a Student Affairs Leadership Program

A preliminary internal review of the student affairs programs identified areas of significant potential for collaboration in the Student Leadership Development Program (SLDP).

The SLDP was a non-credit-bearing program administered by the Office of Student Life. Elements of the program included leadership seminars, community service, and mentoring experiences. The preliminary evaluation found potential in identifying the specific learning objectives and developing appropriate assessment to document students' achievement. The possibility of granting academic credit was raised. At this point the approach turned toward collaboration with the establishment of an advisory committee with representation of faculty and administrators from across the university. The decision to take this approach was based on several factors, including the desire to position the new SLDP as a signature program drawing on the best practices of both student affairs and academic affairs. In addition, an advisory committee with broad representation would set a tone for the project as an inclusive endeavor relating the missions of separate divisions to the mission of the university community.

Although the committee formed specifically to oversee the transformation of the SLDP, the connections and exchanges made among this group had significant effects on the development of other collaborative projects discussed later in this chapter. The result for the SLDP at the end of eighteen months of teamwork was its transformation into the Beacon Leadership Project (BLP), a credit- and competency-bearing program administered as a partnership among the College of Public and Community Service, the Office of Service Learning and Community Outreach, and the Offices of the Deans of Student Affairs and Student Life.

The Framework of Learning Outcomes and the Ways in Which Student Affairs Contributed to the Attainment of Objectives. Undergraduate and graduate students who complete the yearlong program receive two competencies that can be converted into six credits. The BLP is based on the Integrative and Collaborative Learning Model for Student Leadership Development, designed by the assistant dean of students. The model affirms that learning is a shared process in which each individual assumes responsibility for teaching as well as learning. The integrative components focus on engaging students to learn from their own and others' cultures, experiences, ways of knowing, skills, and potentials. Specific learning outcomes are identified in the model and are linked to two competencies: Understanding Social Change Roles through Leadership and Leadership and Community Action. The program involves a seminar series conducted by faculty and student affairs professionals, individualized mentoring partnerships with leaders from within and beyond the university, and service-learning projects. Students have designed such projects as a diversity training in-service workshop for high school teachers, a digital tutoring program for local youth, and a Vietnamese women's group that explores issues of women's identity, roles, and voice through their writing.

Approaches for Developing a Cross-Divisional Partnership. The BLP created a formal and institutionalized partnership between student affairs and academic affairs in large part because of relationships with key individuals in the College of Public and Community Service. Its competency-based programs, emphasis on experiential learning, and commitment to community service distinguish this college. The members of the College of Public and Community Service who served on the advisory committee that created the BLP had expertise in student leadership development and had a common language with student affairs. They took the lead in designing the BLP curriculum and assessment based on the two competencies, Understanding Social Change Roles through Leadership and Leadership and Community Action. Because the College of Public and Community Service already offered these competencies in their programs and had developed effective assessment instruments, the process of gaining approval for the BLP to award academic credit was simplified. These were important considerations in recruiting faculty and administrators from the College of Public and Community Service to serve on the BLP advisory committee.

The story of the advisory committee's formation and its ongoing work is the heart of the discussion on cross-divisional collaboration. This is where the notion of cooperation and "shared ethos of learning" moved from the abstract language of the mission statement to the real work of implementation. In forming the advisory committee, faculty and administrators who were already connected through other committees and initiatives became the foundation for outreach to the academic committee. It was important not only to achieve representation from as many of the colleges and divisions of UMass Boston as possible but also to select individuals who valued the purpose of the endeavor to enhance the learning climate and to develop student leaders. They sought out those who were involved in programs with similar elements, such as the Gastón Institute's Latino Leadership Opportunity Program, and those involved in the burgeoning service-learning programs at the university. A number of those on the BLP advisory committee served simultaneously on an advisory committee for service learning.

Other chapters in this volume have noted that the pedagogy of service learning makes a strong case for connecting the missions of both student affairs and academic affairs and is often an effective locus for collaboration between the two divisions. This was certainly the case at UMass Boston. Not only did the redesign of the leadership program draw on the best practices of service-learning programs, but the process of this collaboration also contributed to the establishment of a new Office of Service Learning and Community Outreach. In recognition of the work of the Service Learning Advisory Committee, the new office was conceived as a unit with oversight of multiple programs and with reporting responsibilities to both student affairs and academic affairs. The organizational diagram of the university now shows this office squarely between student affairs and academic affairs, marking an officially recognized bridge between the divisions.

During the course of the planning process, the BLP advisory committee was designated as a formal advisory board for the program. In addition to student affairs professionals and faculty and administrators from the College of Public and Community Service, the board included representatives from the College of Management, the College of Nursing, Computing Services, and the Office of Service Learning and Outreach. To facilitate cooperation and take advantage of the expertise of the individuals, subcommittees formed to focus on the following areas: program administration and structure (e.g., budget, space, staffing), marketing (e.g., articulating the link to the urban mission of UMass Boston, Web site, publications), and content and resources (e.g., credit and competency program, attention to diversity, guidance for mentors). The Office of the Dean of Students coordinated the long-range planning and maintained contact with each subcommittee. Meetings of the full committee allowed for updates from the subcommittees and discussion, but the bulk of the details were worked out in small-group sessions.

Approaches for Gaining Institutional Support for the Collaboration. The committee worked closely with the university's chancellor and others in executive leadership. All members of the group carefully considered feedback and suggestions. Plans were implemented upon approval, maintaining a sense of productivity and progress. This procedure also meant that the approval and institutionalization of the program did not rest on a single presentation of a proposal at the end of the planning phase. There was "buy-in" from key constituents throughout the process. When the chancellor and provost left their positions a year later, the BLP was fully implemented and touted as one of the university's signature programs. Its stability during the turnover in executive leadership demonstrated the strength of the partnerships and broad base of support. However, those relationships cannot be taken for granted and must be continually tended.

The Diversity Research Initiative: Toward Institutionalization.

The Diversity Research Initiative (DRI) was originally implemented at UMass Boston with the support of a two-year grant from the Ford Foundation and sponsorship by the university's Center for the Improvement of Teaching. Thus it was housed within the Division of Academic Affairs. However, the assistant dean of students learned of the program through his work with faculty and recognized the potential value of linking the DRI to programming in the Division of Student Affairs.

The Framework of Learning Outcomes. One aim of the DRI was "to collaboratively educate and empower undergraduates as investigators of campus diversity, whose data and recommendations educated the university and moved it closer to the goal of inclusion which lies at the heart of UMBs urban mission" (Kingston-Mann, 1999, p. 5). Another aim was to bring the voices of researchers and their subjects from a public, urban, commuter institution into the public conversation on the effects of diversity in higher education. By the end of the two-year funding period, the project yielded thirteen team research projects investigating issues related to the experiences of students in terms of sexual orientation, disability, race, and ethnicity. The program would have ended there except for efforts to institutionalize the DRI as a collaboration between student affairs and academic affairs.

Approaches for Gaining Institutional Support. One of the driving forces toward institutionalization was the ongoing partnership between UMass Boston and the Boston branch of the Office of Civil Rights that focused on enhancing the university's recruitment and retention of minority students. Another was the examination, through the Quality of Life Committee, of the university climate for the learning and development of all students. The Office of the Dean of Students proposed that the DRI could provide ongoing feedback related to the experiences of the increasingly diverse student body and suggested that a joint effort by student affairs and academic affairs could sustain such a program.

Approaches for Encouraging Collaboration. The assistant dean of students wrote a concept paper outlining the goals of the proposed expansion of the DRI and explaining the benefits of a collaborative approach. The paper addressed the director of the Center for the Improvement of Teaching, the provost, and members of the Quality of Life Committee. The following discussion highlights points that could be useful in developing proposals for similar collaborative projects on other campuses.

According to the concept paper, the DRI collaboration between student affairs and academic affairs would serve to

- Promote the ethos of a learning community throughout the university
- Inspire collegiality and communication between the two divisions
- Draw on the expertise of faculty to encourage greater opportunities for undergraduate research
- Draw on the expertise of student affairs professionals to apply research findings directly to promoting student development
- Provide greater opportunities for meaningful connections among students, faculty, and student affairs professionals

The Ways in Which Student Affairs Contributes to the Attainment of the Objectives. The concept paper noted that establishing the initiative as a partnership between student affairs and academic affairs would combine resources of professional expertise and funding from two major divisions. Furthermore, such a partnership would increase the opportunities for obtaining additional funding through professional associations, foundations, and other donors. The addition of student affairs professionals to the research teams would assist in defining questions that have implications for student life and the learning climate. At the same time, the expertise of those in academic affairs related to curriculum design and assessment of learning outcomes would contribute to the effectiveness of student affairs programs responding to research findings. Student affairs would also contribute extensive experience in disseminating information throughout the institution. Such vehicles as seminars, student publications, and student-led workshops could thus present the research findings to a greater audience than would be possible without the participation of student affairs.

At the time of this writing, the DRI is in a pilot program phase with specific faculty who will guide their students in research that is both relevant to the curriculum and to the aims of informing the university about the experiences of students from diverse backgrounds. Discussions have developed regarding the links between the DRI and the new general education curriculum, building a relationship with the Office of Institutional Research, and the need for grants to support and encourage greater faculty participation.

The Beacon Think Tank: From Institutional Mission to Individual Relationships

The Beacon Think Tank (BTT) was designed almost from its conception as a cross-divisional collaboration. Although the design was informed by experiences and models familiar to the coordinators, the think tank did not evolve from an existing program in the way that that the BLP and the DRI did.

The Framework of Learning Outcomes. The BTT is a program of dialogues whose purpose, broadly stated, is to create a climate of reflection and critical thinking that fosters in students a sense of their own citizenship in the university and in society. Think tank members—students who are selected through an application process open to all undergraduate and graduate students—meet about six times during the academic year to discuss issues they feel are the most compelling. Topics have included health care, economic inequalities in the United States, experiences of prejudice, and the financial strains on students at UMass Boston.

The Ways in Which Student Affairs Contributes to the Attainment of the Objectives. The think tank shares many of the learning objectives of the BLP but is distinct from the other program in important ways. As in the BLP, students are accepted based on motivation, leadership potential, and interest in the exploration of societal issues. However, those who choose to participate in the BTT do so on a volunteer basis without academic credit. In fact, many students from the BLP also attend the think tank and inject into the discussions their experiences with internships and leadership-development projects. The think tank creates a space for students to synthesize information from the range of their experiences, including their courses, jobs, cocurricular activities, and life experiences. The facilitation by student affairs staff who know many of the students from different contexts outside of the classroom encourages this. Elements from both the university's mission as an urban, commuter institution and the mission of student affairs informed the list of intended learning outcomes for the think tank experience.

Approaches to Gaining Institutional Support. In the same way as the BLP, the think tank was sparked by the refining of objectives to enhance student learning after the restructuring of the Division of Student Affairs. This development of the BTT highlights the strategies employed to move from divisional or institutional goals to a set of partnerships that make the project come to fruition. The fundamental principle in solidifying this collaborative effort was to provide mutual benefit to the partners while demonstrating the fulfillment of institutional priorities. Because the BTT began as a completely new project, it was set up as a pilot program, which postponed consideration of how to institutionalize it until there was a two-year record to assess.

Approaches to Encouraging Collaboration. The BTT involves collaborations among multiple sectors of the university. Several faculty members serve as advisors to the think tank and were instrumental in designing the program. They represent the College of Public and Community Service and the departments of Critical and Creative Thinking and Psychology. The facilitators of the dialogue, the authors of this chapter, represent the Division of Student Affairs and the New England Resource Center for Higher Education (NERCHE) at UMass Boston. Housed in the Graduate College of Education, NERCHE focuses on collaborative efforts to improve the effectiveness of both policy and practice in higher education. The center is also known for its many think tanks for student affairs and academic administrators.

Conversations with individuals across the campus began shaping the think tank into an active collaboration. Faculty with particular areas of expertise were invited to serve as advisors. The collaborative project offered faculty no explicit rewards from the department or the institution, but those willing to participate shared a commitment to increasing the opportunities for students to engage with issues in meaningful ways.

The primary partnership for the coordination of the BTT was between the Office of the Dean of Students and NERCHE, two units with a shared interest in the method of dialogue as a tool for teaching and learning. For over a decade, NERCHE has convened think tanks for higher education practitioners and facilitated institutional change through processes rooted in collaboration and reflection. The idea of partnering to cofacilitate the think tank developed out of compatible interests. The BTT offered NERCHE a way to hear the students' perspectives on issues. In turn, NERCHE provided a link to a center with established think tank programs and resources. Together, the Office of the Dean of Students and NERCHE could expand the network of professional relationships and resources. For example, NERCHE staff knew faculty in the Department of Critical and Creative Thinking who had particular expertise in guiding students to synthesize and analyze information. Exchanges of information began, and new faculty advisors to the think tank came on board.

A certain creative excitement about shaping a new project maintained the connections among all the partners, although they did not all meet regularly. Two or three would meet for coffee or stop in the hallway to share ideas. These informal sessions strengthened the sense of each person's direct participation in and contribution to the collaboration.

The students were active partners in the development of the think tank. They established consensus about the issues to discuss and offered suggestions about the format and objectives for the year's meetings. They chose to focus on the costs of attending the university and asked questions such as, "What are the most significant expenses? Are there inequalities in how costs impact students? Could we find responsible ways to lower costs?" In teams, the students investigated four areas: health (both the financial costs related to health services and ways to support the health and well-being of students), expenses for books and supplies, transportation costs, and the impact of building a new campus center. Through interviews with various campus officials, literature reviews, and reflections on their own or friends' experiences, they gathered information to present to each other and to spark discussion about the implications of their findings. Some students proposed specific changes in university policy or practice, and the group analyzed the proposals.

The BTT serves as an example of collaboration across divisions and departments that rely on flexible yet functioning partnerships among individuals. The purposeful nurturing of these relationships sustained the project. It is important to point out that all the partners had a vested interest in this project and that its success relied on the extent to which it responded to individual interests while upholding common goals. The rewards for all involved were primarily intrinsic elements related to a sense of accomplishment and excitement about intellectual engagement. This meant that coordinators of the think tank needed to encourage the partners to identify what motivated their participation and then to be attentive to signs of how well the think tank met the partners' expectations. This was especially true for the students because the think tank was created for them. Engaging the students was the primary goal and the ultimate test of success.

Lessons Learned

The lessons learned by the coordinators of these collaborative projects can be divided into two themes: insights about effective collaboration and insights about negotiating the institutionalization of the programs. In both of these areas, communication, through both formal and informal channels, is critical: listening for clues about opportunities, relaying information appropriately, and attending to the self-interests of all parties involved.

A common impetus for collaboration between student affairs and academic affairs is a program review or evaluation that involves the executive leadership of the institution. In the case of UMass Boston, staff turnover triggered a review of the Division of Student Affairs and its relationship to central principles of the university's mission. During the course of program review, the identification of unrealized potential in certain areas creates an agenda for change that could be an opportunity for a collaborative approach. At the same time, the concerns and priorities of institutional leaders often become apparent during discussions of program evaluations, for example, the priority of fulfilling the urban mission of UMass Boston. The recognition by the Divisions of Student Affairs and Academic Affairs of their shared interest in addressing those concerns can form the basis of a partnership. It is important to be attuned to the signals that particular issues are emerging as significant across divisions and then to consider how a potential collaborative initiative might connect with them. The key issues identified at UMass Boston included measurable learning outcomes and addressing the needs of a diverse student population. Faculty, administrators, and staff from across the divisions were expressing their commitment to these issues. This type of agreement is important because it often happens that "hot" topics emerge that may be a priority only to certain well-positioned leaders and may not have broad enough support among faculty and staff to sustain collaboration. Pilot programs such as the BTT are one strategy for testing the support and feasibility of an idea while retaining the option for revising or dismantling the collaboration.

Much of the actual work of collaboration boils down to team building and attending to the individual relationships behind the larger partnerships. Clearly, there are significant challenges in working with the multiple perspectives, priorities, concerns, and personalities of all the stakeholders. Those who operate in a collaborative mode can adjust to present their ideas effectively to different audiences, to interpret both spoken and silent communication, and to negotiate acceptable compromises. A member of the collaborative team's unaddressed concerns can stall the whole project if not dealt with effectively. Mechanisms for feedback need to be part of the system, and stakeholders should feel that they have opportunities to express their ideas or to take the lead in aspects of the project in which they have particular expertise. In the development of the BLP, dividing up the larger team into small task forces proved successfully created manageable feedback loops and opportunities for each member to contribute directly to the project's success.

The variety of perspectives contributed by the collaborating partners, while adding to the challenges, is in fact the most valuable resource of the collaboration. The composition of the team is crucial. Careful consideration should be given to the selection of individuals so that the endeavor has both legitimacy because key leaders are involved and sustainability as a result of the participation of experts and committed people. The nature of the collaborative project may determine who must be on the team, but take advantage of opportunities to consult with others who may have valuable contributions. This could happen through a formal advisory committee or through informal conversations.

Informal and unplanned conversations should not be underestimated. Connections made in conferences, committees, or coffee breaks can sow seeds that grow into a network of relationships and occasionally flower into significant professional partnerships. Such connections are especially valuable when they establish shared interests and mutual respect for each person's expertise. For example, the assistant dean of student affairs at UMass Boston met a number of faculty while participating with them in workshops related to issues of diversity, both on campus and elsewhere. Because they established this initial connection outside of their official roles, they were open to working together later on issues of shared concern. At the same time, sustainable collaborations cannot rely too heavily on the vision or energy of only a few individuals. People may leave for new positions or drop out of an endeavor because they are overextended. The test for a well-functioning team is how well the collaboration can adjust to a certain amount of turnover that is expected to occur.

Finally, there are lessons learned about operationalizing and institutionalizing a collaborative program. Institutional resources and an effective organizational structure must support the teamwork. Although each of the projects discussed in this chapter are cross-divisional collaborations, they are also officially coordinated through an office within the Division of Student Affairs. This provides a straightforward structure for organizing the budgets and lines of accountability. In addition, as the teams developed the initiatives, they took purposeful steps toward institutionalization. First they assessed how the initiative would fit within the existing organizational structures and when necessary, showed how restructuring would advance not only the specific project but also the mission of the university.

A few other strategies already mentioned should be highlighted. In the case of the BLP, lobbying for academic credits and proficiencies was central to the institutionalization of the program. It also helped the success of the BLP and the BTT to develop a polished public relations component with brochures and Web pages. These generated positive attention for the programs and the university.

Conclusion

Building bridges between student affairs and academic affairs requires establishing a common understanding of the learning and developmental outcomes and the ways in which these outcomes will be assessed. In order for the partners to commit to collaboration, they must establish a shared language to articulate how the endeavor will fulfill their commitment to serve the students. Once that foundation has been laid, the work of sustaining and if appropriate, institutionalizing the program begins. As the discussion of the UMass Boston programs has demonstrated, sustainability depends both on the organizational structures and staffing and on the integrity of the collaborative teams. Attention must be paid to both areas. There is no "one-size-fits-all" strategy for successful collaboration because it is a process enmeshed in all the challenges of interpersonal dynamics and shaped by the particular context. Nevertheless, no collaboration is likely to succeed in the long term without open communication and without an organizational structure that supports ongoing teamwork.

References

American Association for Higher Education, American College Personnel Association, and National Association of Student Personnel Administrators. *Powerful Partnerships: A Shared Responsibility for Learning*. Washington, D.C.: American Association for Higher Education, American College Personnel Association, and National Association of Student Personnel Administrators, 1998.

American College Personnel Association. *The Student Learning Imperative: Implications for Student Affairs*. Washington, D.C.: American College Personnel Association, 1994.

Ender, S. C., Newton, F. B., and Caple, R. B. (eds.). *Contributing to Learning: The Role of Student Affairs*. New Directions for Student Services, no. 75. San Francisco: Jossey-Bass, 1996.

Kingston-Mann, E. (ed.). *A Diversity Research Initiative: How Diverse Undergraduate Students Become Researchers, Change Agents, and Members of a Research Community*. Boston: Center for the Improvement of Teaching, University of Massachusetts Boston, 1999.

THARA M. A. FULLER is program coordinator for the New England Resource Center for Higher Education at the University of Massachusetts Boston.

ADRIAN K. HAUGABROOK is the former assistant dean of students at the University of Massachusetts Boston. He is currently the director of Citizen Schools University.

6

Partnerships must not only be created; they must be nourished, sustained, and allowed to evolve.

Lessons Learned: Eight Best Practices for New Partnerships

James Martin and James E. Samels

It is probably safe to say that many readers have by now designed, implemented, or ridden the wave of at least one successful partnership between student affairs and academic affairs on their campuses. However, this chapter is not about those creative efforts. Instead, we focus on how to respond institutionally when a well-planned, high-profile partnership fades, fails, or blows up dramatically—and what best practices can shape a new one from its ashes.

In the course of cowriting an invited paper for the National Association of Student Personnel Administrators, *Building A Better Bridge: Creating Effective Partnerships Between Academic Affairs and Student Affairs* (Martin and Murphy, 2000) and a book on the role of contemporary chief academic officers, *First Among Equals: The Role of the Chief Academic Officer* (Martin and Samels, 1997), we have assessed and helped to design partnership-related projects at more than two dozen institutions over the past decade. As our work progressed, the most thoughtful and difficult questions put to us usually took this form: "We tried a partnership on that issue. It didn't work. What did we do wrong?" Or, "We tried the partnership approach at our institution on several projects, but it never caught on. The members of our team are discouraged. What do we do now?"

Although we quickly learned that there were rarely simple answers for these frustrated colleagues, this chapter identifies eight overarching lessons—and immediate action steps—to build, or rebuild, a successful partnership: (1) be opportunistic, (2) control the budget, (3) capitalize on turnover, (4) avoid collisions of culture, (5) design links to ongoing institutional assessment initiatives, (6) get press, and then get more press,

NEW DIRECTIONS FOR HIGHER EDUCATION, no. 116, Winter 2001 © Wiley Periodicals, Inc.

(7) develop board awareness and support, and (8) don't become attached. In developing these steps, we interviewed a number of people who work in academic and student affairs.

As Deborah Hirsch, director of the New England Resource Center for Higher Education and a coeditor of this volume, has stated, "Partnerships directly reflect, most importantly, successful relationships between the chief student affairs [CSAO] and chief academic affairs officers [CAO]. When a partnership fails, it may not be principally because of the specific event or activity. It may be because the relationship is simply not there between the CSAO and CAO. It is necessary to build that foundation first in order for specific partnerships to succeed."

By the mid-1990s, partnership thinking had created its own literature subset and was emerging in high-profile sessions at numerous national conferences, the American College Personnel Association (ACPA) and the National Association of Student Personnel Administrators (NASPA), especially. By the end of the decade, NASPA, for example, had sanctioned a "Partnership Track" at its annual national gathering with more than forty sessions listed. As the partnership "movement" expanded beyond the two student affairs–oriented national associations to others, including the American Association for Higher Education (AAHE) and the Council of Independent Colleges (CIC), new, complex questions emerged about issues such as partnership authority and accountability.

These lessons reflect new ways to think about partnerships. To start, partnership designers and managers must now approach their objectives more strategically, realizing that whatever the model, the new priorities determining its success will be opportunistic thinking, budget control, turnover impact, cultural compatibility, assessment linkages, and public relations, in roughly that order.

Over the past decade, senior academic and student affairs officers have learned the benefits of thinking more intentionally about partnerships from their outset. Rather than moving narrowly through one partnership at a time, CAOs and CSAOs now link the goals of not just two, but sometimes three or four projects together. In this way, for example, the work of a Joint-Enrollment Task Force can inform the objectives of an Orientation Session on Retention that has been designed to contribute to the agenda of a College-Wide Committee on Student Academic Progress.

These practices reinforce the continuing value and durability of the partnership philosophy while advocating for a more accountable and strategic leadership vision to drive its mission and infrastructure.

Be Opportunistic

It is transcendently important that future partnership models be more fluid and nimble than their predecessors. Rather than wait an extra semester or year for a key faculty member to return from sabbatical, or for senior members of the student affairs team to clear their desk of overdue accreditation surveys, new partnership managers must move beyond all of the reasons to delay action and begin by initiating some basic, modest, and results-oriented joint efforts. As Sheila Murphy, dean for student life at Simmons College, explains, "In the spaces 'between' the traditional partnerships that many are now pursuing, there are usually some excellent, overlooked opportunities that were perhaps not part of an original plan. Instead of responding, 'This doesn't fit our guidelines,' take note of them and realize that the conditions behind these personnel and budget alignments are real and may not appear again for several years. Seize them."

An emerging strategy for many student affairs professionals is to cultivate relationships with colleagues in institutional advancement. Fundraisers who are conversant with an assortment of student affairs priorities and proposed projects can often represent to a donor the value of funding an initiative or idea that an institutional operating budget would be hard pressed to support. The Investment Club at Simmons College is the result of such an initiative. As Murphy describes it, "Starting a new club was not in anyone's plans at the college. In fact, reducing the number of recognized and funded clubs and organizations was an element of the 2001 Strategic Plan for Student Affairs. However, a savvy Major Gifts Officer reflecting on the college's emphasis on the value of cocurricular experiences in 'preparing women for positions of leadership' matched the wishes of a donor whose gift was the result of an exceptionally strong portfolio performance."

The outcome of this opportunistic approach to partnerships, emerging principally from informal conversations and collegiality among staff members in Major Gifts, Student Activities, the Finance Office, and the Student Association, is an Investment Club that annually receives a multithousand dollar gift for investment and that has attracted dozens of students who are both knowledgeable and committed to the economic empowerment of women. Students from Simmons's Graduate School of Management, the only master of business administration program in the nation specifically designed for women executives—many of whom have experience in brokerage houses—advise undergraduates in the club. Faculty members in the finance department have also adapted an offering in their curriculum, Personal Finance and Investing, to include involvement in the club as part of its course requirements.

The Investment Club meets the core criterion for a good partnership: it brings faculty and staff members together in an activity that enhances student learning. Although its development was clearly not in anyone's plans, as Murphy observes, "it became too good an opportunity to let go."

Control the Budget

Partnerships may fade and disappear from a lack of student or faculty interest or from a crippling lack of expertise or planning. However, the greatest source of failure, in our view, continues to be a lack of financial support.

New, more strategic partnership plans avoid this by incorporating control of the budget for that area into the model from its outset to ensure long-term survival.

In order to control the finances for a given area, partnership planners will need to think more creatively about institutional structures and governance. As one example, rather than spending inordinate amounts of time maneuvering through an institution's political channels to gain a sometimes-imperceptible edge in budget influence, simply incorporate the CAO, or that individual's delegate, into the partnership's decision-making matrix. Although the resulting balance, similar to the one evoked in working with trustees, can be a delicate one—"sharing" authority with those holding more of it—experienced managers will also make this trade-off in order to secure the higher level of control.

Roy Austensen, provost and vice president for academic affairs at Valparaiso University for the past ten years, explains the significance of budget control to the success of major institutional partnerships: "The budget is the clincher. Positive rhetoric on partnerships only takes you so far on a campus today. Participants on both sides realize that the imperative is learning, not entertainment, and that much of this learning takes place outside of the classroom. Control of the partnership's budget allows its managers to address this reality by spending strategically and equally to support both sides of the collaboration."

Valparaiso is both a small and complex university. With thirty-seven hundred students and a number of highly regarded specialty programs carrying their own accreditations from agencies such as the National League of Nursing and the American Assembly of Collegiate Schools of Business, the institution works diligently to maintain close attention to each student's academic and personal progress while keeping its overall profile prominent nationally. As Austensen phrases it, "Valpo values community."

As one way to accomplish this, the CAO and CSAO both work on the university's General Education Committee in the refinement of "the Valpo Core," the university's two-semester, ten-hour, first-year program for all entering students. This collaborative model, played out over a period of years, has made the CAO, in Austensen's words, "an advocate for student affairs and all of the associated cocurricular activities within the university. No longer can the CAO stand to one side and simply let the chief student affairs officer be the sole advocate for student affairs at the highest levels of budget discussions and negotiations."

Austensen believes that "CAOs, especially, need to commit to redefining student affairs as a partner with academic affairs in the creation of extraordinary learning environments." At Valparaiso, this continuing commitment has been one of the primary drivers of the increased willingness by the university's Budget Advisory Committee to fund a broad variety of successful partnerships, one of the most prominent being the recrafting of all first-year residence hall programming to support the "Valpo Core" more directly and comprehensively.

Capitalize on Turnover

Even successful partnerships can shine a harsh light on the significant differences in career advancement between tenure-track faculty members and student services professionals. And to the degree, as we argued earlier, that these successful partnerships are relationship-based, perhaps key aspects of the student affairs professional career ladder are inherently problematic and need to be examined for their impact on achieving long-range strategic objectives.

As we noted in *Building a Better Bridge* (Martin and Murphy, 2000), "Career mobility is one of the primary distinctions between student affairs professionals and faculty members, as well as one of the broadest barriers to building long-term successful partnerships. While faculty members seek stability and professional longevity through tenure-track appointments with a clear path to the tenure vote, student affairs professionals are often encouraged to seek new positions every 2 to 4 years in the first decade or so of their careers" (p. 9).

Jean Joyce-Brady, senior associate dean and director of student life at Brown University and a licensed psychologist, offers her perspective on the distance between a faculty member's path to professional achievement and that of a young student affairs professional, as well as the implications of this divide for partnership efforts: "Many overlook the fact that there are *levels* to all partnership projects and programs. The challenge for higher education managers, both faculty and student personnel, is to balance the opportunities in an academic affairs–student affairs partnership with the anxieties experienced when that partnership creates change. Difficult questions from participants, such as, 'Will I lose the opportunity for professional advancement?' and 'Will I have a place in the new structure?' immediately surface." When these opportunities and anxieties are not proactively addressed, it increases the likelihood that the partnership will fail.

Joyce-Brady believes that it is critical to clarify a partnership's global goals when it is originally formed. "With that accomplished, one has the freedom to change formats and systems to address new needs. Most importantly, agreements about global goals should occur first at the senior level of leadership, as this will inform both initial implementation and possible future change at the direct service levels."

As young student affairs professionals seek positions at ever-larger, more prestigious institutions, traditional faculty members continue to view too much career movement as the result of a probable tenure denial or the inability to work with a dean or department chair. Whatever the reasons, it is viewed as a negative and as a failure to join "the academy," a necessity for long-term faculty success.

Eventually, these divergent career paths can defeat a partnership's success. In response, planning teams must proactively confront the possibility that a student union director will leave to work for a major vendor at a higher salary with travel, or that a senior faculty member may resist working with three different resident directors in twenty-four months. However, by treating turnover realistically as a budget tool, partnership managers can leverage these changes into expanded professional development support in the following year as well as into expanded orientation resources and the opportunity to upgrade partnership staff quality through new hires.

Avoid Collisions of Culture

Lori Reesor, assistant dean for the School of Education at the University of Missouri, Kansas City, and formerly dean of students at Wichita State University, connects the success of a partnership with the abilities of its participants to become "other-centered" and to value equally what the other members of the collaboration seek from it. In her experience, a "best practice" is needed to reconcile the differences in career advancement models discussed in the previous section through "skillful effort, extension, and outreach." However, in designing new partnerships with the goal to challenge the institution to become more efficient in serving students and creating stronger learning environments, "tensions can still arise as one team silently and stubbornly continues to believe 'we are not like you.'"

In Reesor's experience, failures of joint ventures between academic affairs and student affairs have occurred because "different cultures were in collision, accompanied by a predictable lack of willingness to understand the other side's objectives—and fears—along with the familiar 'ego factor.'" She provides the following example from her service as dean of students at Wichita State University. The university's student code of conduct had become outdated over the years, and there was a commitment to redesign and modernize its sanctions. Due to changing legal requirements nationwide and an evolving student culture at the university, there was a need for extensive collaboration among students, senior members of the faculty, and student affairs professionals. Although the exercise could have become bogged down or even terminated by conflicting "cultural" responses from those on the faculty and those in student affairs, Reesor describes Wichita State's Code of Conduct Committee as an unqualified success because each group resolved to value the perspectives of the other group to a greater and more visible degree than in previous projects.

By working diligently to incorporate unprecedented levels of communication into the partnership's earliest stages, and by admitting the need for one another's ideas and institutional resources to ensure success over the longer term, the committee through its partnership produced a richer, more flexible document that was endorsed decisively by all three constituencies. One of the principal reasons for this, in Reesor's view, was because "we learned to think more like the 'other' and to foster a sense of trust that continues to exist and to shape policy."

Design Links to Ongoing Institutional Assessment Initiatives

A number of the lessons outlined here can be reduced in concept to that of having the courage and willingness to turn bad news into a fresh start with new tools and personnel. The following lesson, however, comes from a different direction, growing out of nationwide pressures to increase account-ability on all campuses by assessing student outcomes to an unprecedented extent, both in and out of the classroom.

While regional accrediting associations continue to exert a powerful influence on the faculty via national dialogues and summits on the "schol-arship" of teaching, buttressed by massive amounts of material via peer review standards and guidelines, student services professionals have also not been immune to these pressures in their domain.

Savvy student affairs officers learned long ago the wisdom of forging early connections between the objectives of their coventures and the pub-lished outcomes assessment goals of the overall institution. Larry Benedict, dean for student life at the Massachusetts Institute of Technology (MIT) and formerly a senior student affairs officer at The Johns Hopkins University and the University of Massachusetts, provides the following perspective on how partnerships have contributed to, and drawn support from, the cam-pus assessment models he has helped create:

> Almost thirty years ago, when I was at the University of Massachusetts, we established a Student Affairs Research and Evaluation Office expressly for these purposes. That office is still in existence and serving those purposes. What we discovered, among other things, was that student development theory and altruism are clearly important cornerstones of our profession. However, sen-ior level administrators, faculty leaders, key faculty committees, and campus financial planners are much more influenced by comparative data and exter-nal benchmarks than by literature citations, or even worse, by "whining." At the same time, the successful practitioner needs to be savvy enough to know which kinds of data to bring to which collaborators. The kinds of information the senior financial administrator might need or be most influenced by may differ greatly from that requested by the faculty's Curriculum Committee or Grievance Committee.

Benedict has come to believe from his partnerships at the University of Massachusetts, Johns Hopkins, and MIT that both faculty and student devel-opment professionals have gotten distracted in attempting to build joint ventures that carry structure, protocols, and permanent liaisons. In his experience, the most successful partnerships have been "transitory in the sense that faculty, staff, and students have come together to solve a partic-ular problem or develop a specific policy, and then the group has been dis-solved. No matter how much we talk about them and continue to build them, partnerships are still situational, and one needs to bring both the cor-rect data and people to the table to achieve success."

Inadequate academic advising procedures have challenged Benedict's stu-dent affairs team at almost every institution he has served. He believes that no matter the institution's resource base and reputation, "Data demonstrating inadequate academic advising can be used in coordination with the provost or vice president for academic affairs to fund initiatives for improving the advising process, such as a residence hall–based advising program like the one at MIT, or to provide workshops for faculty working with graduate students like those offered at Johns Hopkins. I have seen this work very effectively compared to a simple request for 'more funds' which in competition with all of the other academic sectors can get lost in the shuffle."

Get Press and Then More Press

In earlier years, any press or public relations connected to a partnership initiative was welcome and unexpected. Interviews for a campus newspaper were usually the extent of the story. External coverage was rarely contemplated.

Increasingly, CSAOs and CAOs are not only seeking press coverage for a new orientation and assessment model or a joint-community service program; they are aggressively reaching out to regional news and telecommunications sources while the partnership is still in its *design* stages, taking the strategic perspective that neutral, even negative, coverage can be turned into student awareness and support, followed by a new or expanded budget line in the following year.

As director of campus programs at the University of Maryland, College Park, Marsha Guenzler-Stevens views her role in facilitating partnerships between the university's Offices of Academic Affairs and Student Affairs as conditioned by her ability to shape a stylish and powerful public relations image for each new plan or program: "Good press about partnerships builds a story that reinforces the message of how important it is to engage faculty to an even greater degree in the lives of our students—and it also shows more clearly how to do it. Role modeling is critical. Every time there is a teaching award at the university, our office also tries to distribute a human-interest story from the student development side, such as the career success of a former recipient. This creates a more powerful profile for student affairs as a partner in the press, both internally and externally."

The core question at Maryland is a simple one, Guenzler-Stevens observes: "In one of the country's most media-rich environments, how can we most effectively portray the state's flagship institution, a thirty-four-thousand student, two-thousand faculty member, research-driven enterprise, as humane and caring in and out of its classrooms?" Over the past decade, one key response has been through high-profile partnership projects among the university's Offices of Academic Affairs, Student Affairs, and University Relations.

"Images tell the story," in Guenzler-Stevens's view, and so her office routinely seeks out pertinent Washington and Baltimore major media outlets and specifically invites them to most university events. Whether it is the academically focused "College Park Scholars Service Day" in the fall or the multipurpose "Maryland Day" in the spring, the Office of Campus Programs has benefited significantly by stories and photo opportunities on both cities' nightly newscasts. A prime example of this is "Maryland Day." Originally an idea in the Office of Student Affairs to promote community awareness and involvement, it has grown over the past four years into a festival drawing more than forty thousand participants and requiring a full year to plan.

With everything from science and weather demonstrations to steel drum bands and forums on federal and state education policy, "Maryland Day" incorporates many constituencies from the local community, all alumni, a large contingent of high school junior "prospects," and of course, the media. The event has grown so broad in impact and execution that it is now coordinated by the Office of University Relations on a continuous basis.

Clearly, those who openly court public support for their partnership's objectives will need to manage them carefully and consistently. At the same time, a willingness to share with outside observers strategic thinking early in the design of a partnership, including an acknowledgement of stumbling blocks and pitfalls as well, can be a refreshingly effective strategy. Skillful, public linkages between a partnership's goals and those of the college or university's broader assessment agenda can strike positive chords with chief financial officers, presidents, and the subjects of the next lesson: trustees.

Develop Board Awareness and Support

Develop is meant to imply something stronger than *invite* and less than *expect*. Inviting board of trustee involvement in earlier partnership attempts was easy to do yet hard to accomplish with consistency for extended periods and often of little ultimate consequence.

Positioned as fiduciary stewards with final responsibility for both academic and student affairs, trustees occupy a naturally centered position regarding campus collaborations, and as the baby boom generation moves into retirement, American higher education institutions will be faced with a tremendous turnover in board participation as a younger generation of more technologically literate, dot-com–experienced, volunteers will take their places. These individuals will most likely come from a more diverse variety of livelihoods, and they will be more familiar, via new technologies, with sharing information—and authority—across a greater number of "flat" organizational structures.

Acknowledging that the line between overall policy formulation and daily administration can sometimes become problematically blurred, many experienced CAOs and CSAOs also realize that older, stereotypical approaches to trustee roles lead to stereotypical results. In the next wave of partnerships, board members will be viewed as more active and engaged resources.

Shannon Ellis, vice president for student services at the University of Nevada, Reno and a past national president of NASPA, has gathered extensive experience working with board of trustees at state, regional, and national levels. She provides this primer on how to succeed with trustees when key issues are nearing a vote: "One must be a pragmatist and acknowledge that regents are politicians in their own right and engaged for their own reasons. It is critical to learn those reasons."

Ahead of each upcoming vote, Ellis evaluates the current membership on the board and attempts to identify each regent's agenda for that meeting and how some form of partnership can impact it. One case that demonstrates this point occurred in 1999. Nevada's governor surprised higher education leaders in the state with the introduction of the "Millennium Scholars Program." Through this new program, students who earned a B average in high school would receive most of their tuition covered at a state higher education institution. This translated quickly in the minds of those at the University of Nevada, Reno into a possible rise of 15 percent in student enrollments and a pressing need for more residence space: hence, the creation of their Task Force on Millennium Housing, a partnership-based working group cochaired by Ellis and the university's CAO and populated by key faculty and student affairs personnel, among others.

Understandably, some regents approached a major new building project conservatively, much less its proposed "fast track" for construction over a twelve- to eighteen-month period. To address their concerns, and to achieve the timeline for completion necessary, the cochairs of the task force invited students and parents from the key districts of various regents to the critical board meeting. They then identified each one as a constituent of a regent and asked the students to testify how the new residence hall would allow them to attend the university when it would otherwise not be possible. In the end, the vote was successful and the partnership was viewed as instrumental to achieving this important objective, as both students and regents were included skillfully and centrally in the decision-making process.

In sum, Ellis believes, "It is easy to work with friendly, supportive trustees. It is the ones who think they must be watchdogs for the public every moment who can, sometimes unintentionally, be antagonistic to a new initiative that are the greatest challenge. In those cases, don't be afraid of them and don't avoid them—and give them more time than anyone else."

Don't Become Attached

Throughout the 1990s, the golden rules for partnership managers were short and simple: normalize the model as soon as possible, lock in the budget line immediately, and hire someone to manage it before the end of the semester. Factors such as public relations, board involvement, and outcomes assessment were not priorities for most partnership developers.

The new thinking about partnerships outlined in this chapter is based on a philosophy that argues against permanent, even long-term, arrangements. Planners are encouraged to collaborate on models appropriate to their moment and not to treat those agreements as beyond revision—and dissolution.

As such, partnerships have come to reflect more accurately the evolving missions of their home institutions. Jill E. Carnaghi, assistant vice chancellor for students and director of campus life at Washington University in St. Louis, Missouri, is candid when assessing what lasts about a successful partnership. "Good partnerships have to see beyond themselves and provide each participant with the sense that the bond is more important than the individuals involved. When they are effective, partnerships teach us how to listen to the 'student voice' more clearly than we could before."

But what about a partnership that has outlived its moment and is suffering from declining student and faculty support? Carnaghi is equally direct about addressing this eventuality: "A high profile student affairs–academic affairs partnership is like a marriage. No matter how trite that image continues to sound, if it is no longer working, terminate it so that team members can move on to a new concept, a new team, a new funding source. A partnership needs to be able to continue to identify and address the psychosocial and educational needs of our students, and when a partnership succeeds it is still one of the best ways to create those 'aha!' experiences."

Whether it is in "aha!" moments, in becoming more "other-centered," or in listening more carefully to the "student voice"—while simultaneously maintaining control of its budget, public relations, and staff transitions— student affairs–academic affairs partnerships are now being transformed into more strategic, accountable, and politically savvy identities in order to compete successfully for increased resources and student time amid the many calls for allegiance and engagement on today's campuses.

Finally, partnership managers must act more accountably if for no other reason than that the novelty has worn off the partnership phenomenon, and after fifteen or even twenty years of practice, the stakes have been raised significantly around many projects. Campus planners and budget managers now require a more consistent and measurable return on every partnership dollar commitment.

Among the countless number of partnerships that succeed over the present decade, a new set of lessons will also be learned about how and why some continue to fail. It is our sense that many of these latter lessons can already be viewed in the complex ways our higher education systems develop and preserve inequalities, whether financial, political, or intellectual, between academic and student affairs.

References

Martin, J., and Murphy, S. *Building a Better Bridge: Creating Effective Partnerships Between Academic Affairs and Student Affairs.* Washington, D.C.: National Association of Student Personnel Administrators, 2000.

Martin, J., and Samels, J. E. *First Among Equals: The Role of the Chief Academic Officer.* Baltimore, Md.: Johns Hopkins University Press, 1997.

JAMES MARTIN is a professor of English and former provost at Mount Ida College in Newton, Massachusetts.

JAMES E. SAMELS is president of The Education Alliance, a higher education consulting firm, in Framingham, Massachusetts. Samels and Martin write a column on higher education for the Boston Business Journal.

7

An old campus is revitalized by a new vision for student learning built on student and academic affairs collaboration.

Recentering Learning: An Interdisciplinary Approach to Academic and Student Affairs

Richard Guarasci

Student success occurs within a crucible of good intentions. It requires delicate work, carefully orchestrated to support students, placing learning at the center of campus life. Without an alliance for learning between academic and student affairs, the institutional commitment to student achievement remains disjointed at a minimum, if not shallow in practice.

The landscape of higher education is too often marked by incoherent institutions that are further fractured into separate and competing divisions and departments. On some campuses academic and student affairs operate in distinct realms but within the covenant of an institutional mission and with a shared educational practice. These campuses point us to an emerging educational learning paradigm that reconciles the separation of academic and student affairs. The process starts with clarifying institutional mission and educational goals.

Mission and Goals

Focusing the institutional mission around a learning paradigm means that student and academic affairs units privilege student outcomes over administrative structures. Student-learning outcomes take on a paramount role in organizational design and performance review. Fundamentally, the learning paradigm requires that we ask these essential questions: Do students experience success in gaining skills of inquiry and analysis? Are students gaining mastery within their programs of study? Are students making adequate progress toward their degree? Are the institutional values illustrated in the practice and performance of students?

NEW DIRECTIONS FOR HIGHER EDUCATION, no. 116, Winter 2001 © Wiley Periodicals, Inc.

Figure 7.1. Learning Goals/Cognates

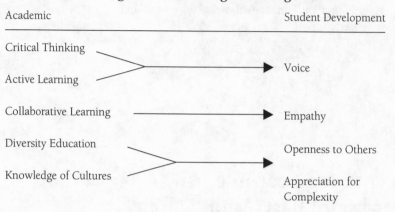

Academic   Student Development

Critical Thinking

Active Learning   Voice

Collaborative Learning   Empathy

Diversity Education   Openness to Others

Knowledge of Cultures   Appreciation for Complexity

By centering educational work on these sorts of questions, faculty members and administrators can find common ground around student success. The learning goals are shared between student and academic affairs, although each may emphasize the different dimensions of any given educational goal. For instance, student-development practice involves significant programs in assisting students in developing "voice," whereas academic affairs prizes the acquisition of critical thinking. The former goal is really a derivative of the latter. Each one has particularities that distinguish it, but they are drawn from a common root of student growth and independent thinking. While classroom pedagogy strongly cultivates active learning, student-development programs aim at building active leadership and campus involvement. Similarly, the goals of diversity education span both domains. As illustrated in Figure 7.1, there is a full range of cognates spanning the intellectual and social development of undergraduate students.

Unfortunately, the organization of university work is designed around a dichotomy that institutionalizes academic learning as if it were apart and separate from the development of self and personality. By identifying common learning goals, we hold open the possibility for approaching both our students and the learning process comprehensively and holistically.

The Need for Common Work

How do we accomplish a sustainable coalition between academic and student affairs? In addition to presidential mandates and organizational reforms, the essential element for reconciliation proves to be nothing less than valued common educational programs.

Our campuses are rich with competing or isolated educational programs that effect student success. We now need to re-envision this work around our common goals through joint programs. The most promising candidates are diversity education, community-based learning, residential curricular programs, and first-year and senior-year programs. To be successful, each of these initiatives requires strong alliances between several administrative offices. Each contains elements for higher campus involvement by students, which is a strong influence on student success.

Diversity Education

When done well, diversity programs teach students the skills of democratic leadership that help them learn how to bring people together across differences. By engaging both the history of cultural specificity and the psychosocial dynamics of prejudice, hierarchy, and patriarchy, successful diversity education provides student learners with more than a vocabulary of difference. These programs equip students with multiple attachments among many other students and reaffirm a sense of purposeful identity on the campus.

Successful diversity programs require sharp interdisciplinary alliances between faculty and student affairs participants in forging curricular and cocurricular contributions for comprehensive learning. The University of Michigan's Intergroup Dialogue Program is a stellar example of one such success. It is composed of a highly sophisticated cocurricular program on campus and within residential life while integrated into a variety of full-credit courses. The program works so well, and with great national recognition, in part because of the delicate collaboration among faculty members, administrators, and student trainers.

Community-Based Learning

For service- or community-based learning programs, academic and student affairs offices need to work in close contact with faculty members and community organizations. Students involved in community-based learning can make critical connections between classroom texts and field experience in the community. In numerous cases, this type of program connects students with traditional academic classes in powerful ways and with improved academic performance as measured along standard educational success measures.

In these programs, course syllabi include assignments and classroom discussions of students' fieldwork. Careful coordination is required between faculty members and the offices for experiential learning and community service in arranging site locations, field assessments, transportation and overall coordination. Successful community-based learning programs develop course work around shared learning goals.

Recently, one of my students engaged in a community-based learning course discussed how she discovered much about herself as a result of her engagement in deep community activity: "Through all of the readings and service, I discovered the extraordinary possibilities within myself. . . . Although this redefinition of self was frightening and frustrating, it seemed to rob me of stability and certainty, I like [Audrey] Lorde, 'began to recognize a source of power within myself that comes from the knowledge that while it is most desirable not to be afraid, learning to put fear into a perspective gave me great strength'" (Guarasci and Cornwell, 1997, pp. 44–45).

Community-based learning maintains experiential possibilities for the integration of student-identity formation, campus connection, and civic participation. This combination is a powerful one for student success and requires that student and academic affairs work together around shared learning goals and with a common reflective practice.

Residential Colleges

Probably the most thorough academic and student affairs collaborations occur within "living and learning" programs that join together academic courses with residential life. As sophisticated as any, St. Lawrence University's first-year program houses all first year students together while they are simultaneously enrolled in a two-semester interdisciplinary core course. Three faculty members teach in each of the dozen or so sections, and all three share an office within the allied residence (in addition to their departmental offices). Joined by residence directors within the dormitories, the faculty and residence hall staff link the course content with hall programming drawing out the larger issues of community, identity, governance, gender, race, class, and ethnicity from within the direct experience of communal living. For example, texts on issues of diversity, difference, and community relate directly to the coeducational multiethnic and racial issues within the residence hall. Issues as simple as deportment involve sharp debates on shared responsibilities. Canonical and contemporary texts within the traditional liberal arts speak to those questions, allowing linkages between classroom experiences and residence hall discussions. Academic growth and student development are approached in a holistic pedagogy that provides faculty and student affairs participants with the opportunity for a powerful program linking intellectual and social issues around values, ethics, and morals.

The St. Lawrence program links academic advising, first-year curriculum, residential life, and student activities. It is a powerful model for integrated work focused on student learning and academic success.

First-Year and Senior-Year Programs

At Wagner College in New York City, both first-year and senior-year programs rely on learning communities, experiential learning, and reflective practice to link learning across the boundaries of the curriculum, academic advising, residential life, and career development. All first-year students enroll in a three-course learning cluster involving full three-credit (one unit) courses, all meeting general education distributions and integrated around a common theme. For instance, one of the more than twenty first-year-program learning clusters links a common cohort of students around the theme of "The City and Civilization" in the Western Civilization course with the Western Literature course (twenty-eight students). These courses focus on ancient Athens and Rome, medieval Paris, Renaissance Florence, and contemporary New York City. In a third course, a reflective tutorial, students read further on the basic theme. They are assigned and mentored in a series of research writing events, culminating in two drafts of a first college paper. Finally, students complete thirty hours in community settings directly related to the course themes. Students are asked to compare and contrast the course texts and fieldwork through reflective writing and discussion assignments.

Academic advising, the writing center, residential life, experiential learning, and career development are other components within Wagner's first-year program. The program's full impact is demonstrated by the enhanced academic success of first-year students. The college's first-year retention rate improved by twelve percentage points to 85 percent. The program is a model for successful collaboration across both academic and student academic affairs.

Wagner College's senior-year program requires a learning community within the major discipline for all senior students, linking a capstone course, senior thesis, and reflective tutorial with mover than one hundred hours of experiential learning. The senior-year program is based on the single goal of helping students to answer the question, "What does it mean to be a reflective practitioner within this discipline?" Here, too, the advising, experiential learning, and career development offices are joined in a powerful collaboration with the academic departments.

Building and Sustaining Campus Collaboration: A Case Study from Wagner College

As late as 1997, Wagner College provided a fairly typical example of an institution organized into administrative and departmental campus silos. By 2001 it was recognized in its regional ten-year reaccreditation visitor's report by the Middle States Commission on Higher Education as a model of collaboration and interdisciplinarity across the entire campus and a coherent, focused, and learning-centered educational institution. It provides us with a case study for examining the critical issues and relationships involved in building and sustaining campus collaboration for institutional transformation.

Wagner College is located on Staten Island, the smallest of New York City's five boroughs. Founded in 1883, as Wagner Lutheran College, the college offered bachelor's degrees in 1928 and became a coeducational institution in the early 1930s. In 1958 it was renamed Wagner College, and in the 1960s it ended any formal relationship with the Lutheran Church. In 2001 only 1 percent of the college's students refer to themselves as Lutheran, and close to 50 percent identified themselves as Catholic.

Today the college enrolls over seventeen hundred full-time, traditional-aged undergraduates and approximately three hundred graduate students spread across seven master's degree programs. Over 75 percent of undergraduates are resident students housed in the 105-acre bucolic campus located on Grymes Hill overlooking Manhattan and the New York Harbor.

For most of its existence since 1918, Wagner students came from the local surroundings of Brooklyn, Staten Island, and nearby New Jersey. Even as late as 1997, close to 50 percent of the undergraduates came from the New York metropolitan area. By 2001 only 25 percent of undergraduates were "metro" students, and close to 60 percent of recent entering classes have come from outside of New York State, with the majority of students from New England, Pennsylvania, and the Midwest with a growing contingent from throughout the United States, particularly California. A summary of the characteristics of the student population in 1990–91 and in 2001–02 highlights the dramatic changes that have taken place at Wagner College (see Table 7.1).

In 1987 Wagner College was close to ceasing operations. Enrollment had fallen off dramatically. Full-time faculty was reduced by over 50 percent. The college was running a chronic deficit and had a small endowment. The Financial Aid Office was discounting tuition and fees by over 50 percent. The campus was in physical disarray.

A new president was hired at that time, and in five years he reordered the physical campus, refinanced the debt, and established a run of balanced budgets. He also moved to integrate administrative services. In 1997 he hired a new provost, who helped the faculty to invent The Wagner Plan for the Practical Liberal Arts, a four-year comprehensive educational signature for the entire undergraduate program. By 2000 *U.S. News and World Report* ranked Wagner College in its top tier of northeast colleges and universities. In 2000 the Association of American Colleges and Universities identified Wagner College as having one of the most innovative and promising undergraduate curricula in the United States. And in fall 2001, *Time* named

Table 7.1. Demographics of Wagner College

	AY 1990–91	AY 2001–02
Undergraduate enrollment (full-time equivalent)	1,117	1,720
SAT profile	812	1,120
Resident students	586	1,200
Geographical distribution: Percentage of New York City metro students	69%	25%
Total full-time faculty	69	100
Faculty (full-time equivalent)	80	120

Wagner College as one of its colleges of the year for its first-year program ("*Time*'s Colleges of the Year," 2001).

All of this suggests that Wagner College's success has followed from a clear mission built around student success within a coherent, understandable, and focused educational program—the Wagner Plan—that revitalizes liberal education around experiential and community based learning. There is great pride and accomplishment among the faculty and students. Finally, the financial health of the college is ensured by an involved and highly enthusiastic family of stakeholders—trustees, alumni, parents, and the local Staten Island community. Wagner's seventeen hundred undergraduates contribute over fourteen thousand hours annually in experiential and community-based learning directly and integrally related to clusters of courses within learning communities.

How was this built, sustained, and nurtured? What obstacles were encountered, overcome, and still remain?

Building and Sustaining Collaboration

Central to all change, a clear and compelling educational plan requires a sensible vision of student success. Stated more conventionally, an educational vision of a learning-centered campus is a paramount component for institutional change.

Part of such a vision establishes a set of responsibilities for campus leadership. Without an experienced, highly energized senior leadership team, campus collaboration becomes problematic. The leadership model needs to be appropriate to the campus culture(s) and heritage. In the Wagner College case, leadership style from 1997 forward was based on the assumption that strong leaders need strong publics to realize the full potential of the institution. We might call this the "thick" model of participatory leadership, in which faculty, administrators, trustees, parents, students, and the local community have a great deal of information, knowledge, and involvement in campus decision making.

The second element in collaboration is similar to the pedagogy of the engaged classroom. Active and collaborative learning requires students who are involved in dialogue, debate, cooperative problem solving, and experiential, community-based learning. Students develop a sense of voice and learn the art of dialogue, mediation, and connection. The end result often is greater learning and enhanced student achievement, and so too, with campus leadership. Campus stakeholders need leader-teachers who are self-confident with the engaged campus. They need to be comfortable with the rich variety of campus personalities and individual temperaments. They need to encourage and welcome differences, and most important, they need to focus the entire campus on the one unimpeachable goal of the mission—student learning.

This type of leadership, like this type of classroom teacher, will inspire, motivate, cajole, challenge, and integrate the various administrative and faculty personalities into a larger commitment to student learning. These leaders will reshape the reward and resource systems to support this goal by demonstrating it in appointment, renewal, tenure, and promotion decisions of the faculty. They will reward participating administrators. They will construct budgets so that resources flow toward these ends. They will communicate clearly and often with students, parents, and the other stakeholders.

In short order the obstacles to change—limited resources, fatalistic campus cultures, fear and suspicion of administrative authority—will transform into issues and problems to be discussed, engaged, and solved through reflective practice.

At Wagner College the change was deep and quick. Trust and innovation became soul mates. Involvement has a way of converting problems from external constraints into personal challenges. But clearly, the largest obstacle remains resource shortage. There is never enough funding for facilities to achieve everything. One case in point is transportation to support the vast movement of seventeen hundred students into Manhattan, Brooklyn, New Jersey, and across Staten Island to support experiential learning. At Wagner the provost's office created a new section with clerical support for student placement linked closely to course assignments. Vans were needed to literally move people from campus to public transportation. Creative budget management, reprogramming of resources, and a few key appeals for grant support solved these problems. In fall 1997 not many believed it possible to support seventeen hundred students involved in fourteen thousand hours of experiential learning. Today it is an accepted part of normal business.

Faculty-development workshops, external funding, stipends for involved faculty members, intelligent hiring practices that find new hands committed to institutional change around the mission, student briefings, full and frequent communication, accountable management, open campus meetings, outside consultants, external validation: all of these elements are the muscle and tissue of establishing and nurturing campus collaboration. Clearly, new interdisciplinary administrative structures will follow, and they need to be incorporated formally into the formal governance system. But the Wagner case demonstrates that the critical element remains—involvement, dialogue, problem posing, and purposeful action form the core of participatory and collaborative leadership in the classroom as well as across the campus. Success will follow.

Toward a Transformative Model of Learning

The learning model focuses campus work on the question, "Who are our students becoming?" It requires the restructuring of the traditional organization of campus and professional work. Collaborations among various academic and student affairs units are necessary but insufficient in and of themselves. What is required is a wholesale rethinking of our respective responsibilities grouped now around student learning and success.

If we seek active and collaborative learning classrooms, then we need administrative pedagogies that accentuate the same values. In some rough analogy, we need to be asking ourselves, "Who are we becoming professionally?" William Sullivan's recent book *Work and Integrity* (1995) discusses this very point. Sullivan argues that all professionals need to link their work closely to the needs of the communities they serve. For higher education, our overriding professional work is student learning. Independent of organizational specification and our particular portfolio responsibilities, the larger institutional rationale for our professional duties is the educational success of our students. To accomplish this end, higher education administration needs its own interdisciplinary structures focused on student learning across the campus. In the end, institutional coherence requires a new model of educational leadership at all levels of the organization. These new leaders, like our students, will need to learn the skills of collaboration, negotiation, mediation, coalition, and purposeful action. Our students' success depends on it.

References

Guarasci, R., and Cornwell, G. *Democratic Education In An Age of Difference: Redefining Citizenship in Higher Education.* San Francisco: Jossey-Bass, 1997.

Sullivan, W. *Work and Integrity: The Crisis and Promise of Professionalism in America.* New York: HarperCollins, 1995.

"*Time*'s Colleges of the Year." *Time,* Sept. 10, 2001, pp. 64–74.

RICHARD GUARASCI *is the provost and vice president for Academic Affairs at Wagner College. He holds the rank of professor of Political Science and teaches in the areas of democracy, citizenship, and American diversity.*

8

*The creation of a brand-new college of engineering was as
an opportunity to rethink the curriculum and
cocurriculum and the interaction between the two.*

Building the Foundation for Collaboration: Seamless Learning at a New College

Rod Crafts, Zachary First, and Jeffrey Satwicz

In the mid-1990s, business leaders and the National Science Foundation called for major changes in the way engineers were being educated. Recommended changes included an increased emphasis on business and entrepreneurship, teamwork, communication skills, and interdisciplinary design while maintaining a rigorous preparation in the fundamentals of engineering and science. Although many engineering schools began taking incremental steps to adjust to changing demands, the F. W. Olin Foundation believed that the best approach was to start with a clean slate and create a totally new engineering college that would immediately incorporate all of the needed changes. The Commonwealth of Massachusetts chartered the Franklin W. Olin College of Engineering on November 18, 1997, officially beginning a forty-five-month strategic planning process.

The new college opened its doors to thirty Olin Partners on August 23, 2001. The Olin College Mission Statement (2001) reads, "The founding principle of the Franklin W. Olin College of Engineering is to prepare leaders able to predict, create and manage the technologies of the future. Olin education will be provided at little or no cost to bright, talented, creative, and ambitious students, regardless of their financial circumstances. The faculty, curriculum, and facilities will be unsurpassed and deliberately designed for fast and continuous change to adapt to technology and meet the business needs of the twenty-first century."

The student partners, including coauthor Jeffrey Satwicz ('06), are to spend the 2001–02 academic year helping create this new college. Exemplifying their generation of high-achieving team players known as "millennials" (Lowery and Strauss, 2001), the students will work with the faculty in designing and testing the curriculum, assist the student life staff in shaping student life and policies, and serve as ambassadors for the college in the admission process for the remainder of the first official class, which will arrive in 2002. In this new student-centered setting with the previously cited goals, how should the founding administrators, faculty, and students set the stage for a healthy collaboration between academic affairs and student life at Olin College?

To Whom Should the Chief Student Affairs Officer Report?

Early in the brief history of Olin College, the trustees and senior officers decided that the chief student affairs officer (to be titled dean of student life) would report to the provost. The dean would serve on the president's seven-member leadership team with the provost, the vice president for administration and finance, the vice president for innovation and research, the vice president for external relations and enrollment, and the dean of admission. Areas under the jurisdiction of the dean of student life would include the academic-advising support structure, student activities, residence life, new-student orientation, the disciplinary system, athletics and intramurals, health services, psychotherapy and psychiatric services, spiritual life, international student services, and the registrar. Olin will share some of these services with neighboring Babson College and will contract with off-campus consultants for other services.

Coauthor Rod Crafts was attracted to the dean of student life position for all of the obvious reasons, including the excitement of helping to shape a new college, designing student life from a clean slate, and recruiting the college's first student life administrative team. As important as any other factor was the reporting line to the provost. After thirty years as a student affairs professional, Crafts had found that forming and maintaining solid relationships with faculty was both more important and more elusive than establishing ongoing relationships with colleagues in other areas of the administration (e.g., business affairs, development, admissions). Although reporting to the president may appear to involve more "power," the ability to get things done and influence the life of the campus are outgrowths of healthy day-to-day relationships. Reporting to the provost puts the dean in closer proximity to the faculty, to the curriculum, and to the intersection of the curriculum and cocurriculum.

A Two-Way Street with the Faculty

During the planning year 2000–01, the dean's reporting relationship to the provost provided several opportunities to cultivate healthy working relationships with faculty. Asked to design the Partner Year schedule, the dean consulted each of the nine inaugural faculty members before presenting a series of drafts at faculty and leadership team meetings. The dean was included in faculty retreats at which short- and long-term curriculum planning was conducted and was asked to organize and schedule opportunities for the partners to work with individual faculty in developing curriculum and academic-enrichment offerings. Unlike the customary student affairs role as "the supervisor of nonacademic services," the dean's role at Olin College has been one of faculty colleague.

As a by-product of the dean's relationships with faculty, he was able to recruit faculty volunteers for seven faculty-staff teams that focused on the following: planning the new-student orientation program, residence life, the honor code and student disciplinary system, spiritual life, the creative arts program, the community-service program, and selecting a book for student summer reading. In turn, the dean and assistant dean were easily able to include faculty in establishing the orientation schedule, determining initial residence hall policies, researching honor code issues, visiting the local clergy association, and in negotiating ideas for community-service projects with Needham School System administrators and other community leaders. Whereas involving faculty in "out-of-class" life seems a struggle on most established campuses, the traditional line between the curriculum and cocurriculum has been intentionally blurred at Olin College.

Making the College Attractive to New Staff

Coauthor Zachary First joined the Olin College staff on June 1, 2001, fresh from receiving his master's degree in education at the Harvard University Graduate School of Education. He accepted the position of assistant dean of student life with the understanding that work in student life at Olin would be closely connected with that of the faculty. For a young professional just out of graduate school, this was an all-too-rare opportunity to carry on the big thinking of the classroom in the day-to-day operations of an actual college. Unencumbered by the traditional student affairs–academic affairs split, Olin promised the chance to pioneer a working relationship with faculty and fellow administrators in which previously unattainable ideas might be made reality.

Olin is delivering on this promise because it was designed with the understanding that a successful merger of student and academic affairs would require more than a realignment of the institution's organizational chart. Student life staff and faculty must come to see themselves as engaged in a common enterprise, and such cooperation depends on their ongoing involvement in everyday learning opportunities: team teaching, curriculum decisions, assessing student outcomes (Price, 1999). Olin both provides these everyday opportunities and visibly promotes them by intermingling traditionally segregated spaces such as classrooms, administrative offices, and faculty offices (Price, 1999).

Less than one year into his job, Olin's new assistant dean has found that the planned integrated environment is a reality. He is, for example, in demand as a team teacher and an instructor in Olin's burgeoning cocurricular program, in which faculty and staff provide opportunities for learning outside of the classroom and lab. In return for his time and energy spent working in partnership with the academy, the assistant dean has found his requests for faculty participation in designing and supporting many aspects of campus life met with an equal measure of enthusiasm and commitment. The belief that student learning stems not solely from courses but also from interdependent intellectual and social experiences that occur both inside and outside the classroom (Kuh, 1996) has allowed faculty and student life professionals to coordinate in- and out-of-class learning experiences. Combined, they create a whole out of the traditionally faculty-valued developmental outcomes (intellectual) and the traditionally student affairs–valued outcomes (affective and moral) that is greater than the sum of its parts (Banta and Kuh, 1998).

Making the College Attractive to Students

Coauthor Jeffrey Satwicz turned down offers of admission to well-established top-ranked research universities in order to become part student, part educational consultant in establishing a new engineering college. He knew that Olin's small size meant that he would receive the kind of personal attention that would have been impossible at another college. He also knew that as a start-up school, Olin would provide a canvas for his numerous ideas about how to shape the college experience.

Even with all of the expected bumps in the road, Satwicz believed that the close cooperation of Olin's faculty and staff would result in a smooth educational experience and that the communication among the various disciplines and between the faculty and administration would be the key to this cooperation. He saw no reason for student life and academic life to come into conflict and believed that as long as both were willing to work together, communicate, and compromise, there should be no tension. Although Satwicz knew that creating a revolutionary curriculum would be difficult, he suspected that incorporating extracurricular activities into traditional academic learning would be revolutionary in itself.

In high school Satwicz learned most in the classes in which he had the most fun. The blend of academics and extra- and cocurricular activities at Olin makes learning more enjoyable and more pervasive and will ensure that Satwicz and his fellow students have many more opportunities to learn than would otherwise be possible.

Maintaining the Partnership

The building blocks are now in place at Olin College for a smooth working relationship between the student life staff and the faculty. Still, as the campus grows over the next decade from its present state with 15 faculty and 30 students to its goal of 650 students and 65 faculty, the increase in size will challenge this budding partnership. What techniques are Olin's student life administrators considering to maintain the mutually beneficial relationship?

Administrators will encourage student-life staff to

- Stay involved in faculty recruitment, attend candidate presentations, and interview each candidate about their "student life philosophy" focusing attention at this stage in order to provide lasting memories for new faculty recruits
- Attend faculty meetings as regularly as possible and contribute to the discussion on issues beyond student life
- Socialize informally with faculty (e.g., potluck dinners, celebrations, and special occasions)
- Organize campus-wide programs and events that emphasize faculty involvement (e.g., speakers, open forums, dialogues on world events)
- Regularly visit faculty in their offices and labs
- Ask faculty to cosponsor on-campus symposia by nationally known higher education researchers (e.g., campus culture, honor codes, legal issues)
- Engage faculty in dialogues about student life policies for residence halls, controversial speakers, crisis response, athletics, etc.
- Provide budgetary support for faculty to interact with students outside the classroom (e.g., pizza and soda for a discussion at a faculty member's home, tickets to a museum or play, transportation to an historic site)
- Recognize faculty contributions during the promotion process, through articles in the campus newsletter or items on the campus Web site, and through "professor-of-the-semester" awards

Faculty would be expected to

- Participate in student events and programs whenever possible
- Invite student life administrators to participate in class discussions, coteach class sessions, or serve as coresearchers
- Socialize informally with administrators
- Regularly visit administrators, with or without an issue or agenda, in their offices
- Stay involved in student life administrator recruitment, attending candidate presentations

Finally, administrators would encourage students to

- Learn about faculty, administrators, and staff as "real people" beyond their campus roles
- Regularly visit faculty and administrators, with or without an issue or agenda, in their offices
- Invite faculty, administrators, and staff to student-initiated receptions

- Recognize faculty contributions to the student life program
- Stay involved in student life administrator recruitment, attending candidate presentations

Institutionalizing the Academic Affairs–Student Life Connection

Among the many lessons learned thus far in the development of the academic affairs–student life partnership at the Olin College of Engineering, the following are the most striking:

- Faculty members realize they are not student life experts and are naturally reluctant to plunge into student life without being asked. Regular invitations from student life staff are necessary and appreciated.
- Student life staff should not treat their relationship with faculty as a one-way street, expecting faculty involvement without offering assistance with, for example, curricular issues.
- Faculty are more likely to respond in kind to the curricular contributions of student life staff by volunteering to assist with student life programs and events when relationships with the student life staff are individually cultivated from their first days on campus.
- If skilled and astute, student life staff can serve as the "glue" of the campus. Shuttle diplomacy among faculty, between faculty and other administrators, and between faculty and students is an unrecognized talent of most student fife administrators and can be cultivated if solid relationships are maintained. Other senior administrators need to tolerate student life staff crossing organizational boundaries to perform this "sticky" function.

Sustaining and Deepening the Academic Affairs–Student Life Connection

With Olin's culture and structure still in the early stages of development, it is impossible to predict how the academic affairs–student life connection will change and grow in coming years. Still, the strategic planning years and the Partner Year have given the college a solid foundation for a rich and productive collaboration. As a result, several of its current practices, including soliciting and offering involvement and contributions in both student life and academic affairs areas, may grow into principles around which our working lives are structured. Whatever the future details of the partnership may be, continued success most certainly depends on both student life and academic affairs staff remaining flexible to unanticipated outcomes, new approaches, and the renewing upheaval wrought by cooperation.

References

Banta, T. W., and Kuh, G. D. "A Missing Link in Assessment: Collaboration Between Academic and Student Affairs Professionals." *Change,* 1998, *30*(2), 40–47.

Kuh, G. D. "Guiding Principles for Creating Seamless Learning Environments for Undergraduates." *Journal of College Student Development,* 1996, *37*(2), 135–148.

Lowery, J. W., and Strauss, W. "The Millennials Come to Campus." *About Campus, 6*(3), 2001, 6–12.

Olin College Mission Statement. [http://olin.edu/overview/mission.html]. September 17, 2001.

Price, J. "Merging Student Affairs with Academic Affairs: A Promotion or Demotion for Student Affairs?" In J. H. Schuh and E. J. Whitt (eds.), *Creating Successful Partnerships Between Academic and Student Affairs.* New Directions for Student Services, no. 87. San Francisco: Jossey-Bass, 1999.

ROD CRAFTS is dean of student life at the Franklin W. Olin College of Engineering.

ZACHARY FIRST is assistant dean of student life at the Franklin W. Olin College of Engineering.

JEFFREY SATWICZ is an Olin Partner and member of the graduating class of 2006 at the Franklin W. Olin College of Engineering.

INDEX

Back Issue/Subscription Order Form

Copy or detach and send to:
Jossey-Bass, A Wiley Company, 989 Market Street, San Francisco CA 94103-1741

Call or fax tollfree: Phone 888-378-2537 6AM-5PM PST; Fax 800-605-2665

Back issues: Please send me the following issues at $27 each

(Important: please include series initials and issue number, such as HE114)

1. HE _____

_____

_____

$ _____ Total for single issues

$ _____ SHIPPING CHARGES: SURFACE

	Domestic	Canadian
First Item	$5.00	$6.50
Each Add'l Item	$3.00	$3.00

For next-day and second-day delivery rates, call the number listed above.

Subscriptions: Please ❑ start ❑ renew my subscription to *New Directions for Higher Education* for the year 2____ at the following rate:

U.S.	❑ Individual $60	❑ Institutional $131
Canada	❑ Individual $60	❑ Institutional $171
All Others	❑ Individual $84	❑ Institutional $205

$ _____ Total single issues and subscriptions (Add appropriate sales tax for your state for single issue orders. No sales tax for U.S. subscriptions. Canadian residents, add GST for subscriptions and single issues.)

Federal Tax ID 135593032   GST 89102 8052

❑ Payment enclosed (U.S. check or money order only)

❑ VISA, MC, AmEx, Discover Card # _____ Exp. date_____

Signature _____ Day phone _____

❑ Bill me (U.S. institutional orders only. Purchase order required)

Purchase order #_____

Name _____

Address _____

_____

Phone_____ E-mail _____

For more information about Jossey-Bass, visit our Web site at: www.josseybass.com

PROMOTION CODE = ND3